WOOD Magazine®

Router Tips, Jigs & Techniques

Edited by Peter J. Stephano

STERLING PUBLISHING CO., INC.
NEW YORK

Library of Congress Cataloging-in-Publication Data

Wood® magazine router tips, jigs & techniques / edited by Peter J. Stephano
    p. cm.
 Includes index.
 ISBN 1-4027-0752-5
 1. Routers (Tools) 2. Joinery. 3. Jigs and fixtures. I. Title: Router tips, jigs & techniques. II. Better homes and gardens wood.

TT203.5.W66 2003
684'.083--dc22   2003056858

10 9 8 7 6 5 4 3 2 1

Published by Sterling Publishing Co., Inc.
387 Park Avenue South, New York, NY 10016
© 2005 by Meredith Corporation
Distributed in Canada by Sterling Publishing
c/o Canadian Manda Group, 165 Dufferin Street
Toronto, Ontario, Canada M6K 3H6
Distributed in Great Britain by Chrysalis Books Group PLC
The Chrysalis Building, Bramley Road, London W10 6SP, England
Distributed in Australia by Capricorn Link (Australia) Pty. Ltd.
P.O. Box 704, Windsor, NSW 2756, Australia

Printed in China

Sterling ISBN 1-4027-0752-5

For information about custom editions, special sales, premium and corporate purchases, please contact Sterling Special Sales Department at 800-805-5489 or specialsales@sterlingpub.com.

Acknowledgments

The greatest appreciation goes to the past and present design and editorial staff of Meredith Corporation's *Better Homes & Gardens*® *WOOD*® magazine for the technical advice, projects, tips, and techniques that you'll find in this book. A very special thanks also to craftsmen Kevin Boyle, Jim Downing, Chuck Hedlund, and Jan Svec for their expertise and ingenuity in creating much of the material in this book. Individual project designers are also noted as appropriate.

Finally, my gratitude to Administrative Assistant Sheryl Munyon at *WOOD* magazine; Jackie Keuck, Meredith's Art Library Manager; and Bob Furstenau, head of Meredith's Information Systems and Technology department, for their efforts in helping assemble the material.

Peter J. Stephano

Table of Contents

Introduction

The Router: an essential power tool

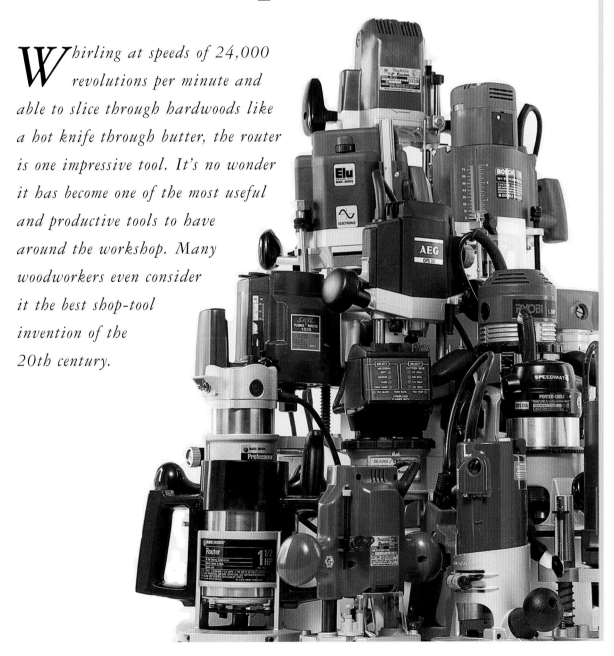

*W*hirling at speeds of 24,000 revolutions per minute and able to slice through hardwoods like a hot knife through butter, the router is one impressive tool. It's no wonder it has become one of the most useful and productive tools to have around the workshop. Many woodworkers even consider it the best shop-tool invention of the 20th century.

The first commercially manu-factured router was intro-duced near the end of World War I, the invention of a New York patternmaker who creat-ed it by reworking a barber's clipper. Surprisingly, the router's basic design has changed very little since then. Current models, although they may look more trendy and carry some new-fangled features, still work essentially the same way as their earliest counterparts. Only the plunge router, a rather recent devel-opment, shows any significant design evolution.

Pick up any modern router and you'll find the same three basic elements—a high-speed electric motor attached to a base, a height-adjusting mech-anism to raise and lower the motor within the base, and a special chuck or collet fitted to the motor shaft to hold the cutting bits. Router bits, while also similar to the few early offerings, are now available in hundreds of styles, shapes, and sizes, as you'll discover in Chapters 5 and 6 of this book.

A tool with many advantages

In the workshop, routers per-form two primary tasks, but cutting decorative edges on boards is by far the most com-mon. Shaping the edge of a workpiece adds a finishing touch and transforms an ordi-nary-looking project into an attractive one that catches the eye faster than any other sin-gle thing you could do.

The router's lesser-known role is for cutting joints when assembling furniture and other woodworking projects. More and more woodworkers today are finding the router indispensable in this capacity. In Chapter 2, you'll discover a number of other things you can do with a router as well as some valuable techniques to upgrade your woodwork-ing skills.

The router's success as a common woodworking power tool can be attributed to the fact that there are a number of inherent advantages it has over other tools. Its small size and unique design enable it to do jobs that no other tool can.

Its duplicating capability also allows you to complete many operations easier, faster, and more safely than with other tools.

You can't beat a router for portability, either—you can carry and use it almost anywhere and get accurate results every time. Compare that with other cutting tools, such as a shaper or tablesaw!

Because it's portable, it will work on virtually any size stock, eliminating workpiece-size restrictions and limitations common to many machines. And most importantly, you'll find today's routers still modestly priced compared to many other machines of comparable capability or capacity. Plus, if you mount this normally handheld tool beneath a table, as you'll discover in Chapters 3 and 4, you'll transform it into a still *more* versatile machine.

Putting your router to work

Routers are actually very simple machines, but don't let their simplicity fool you—they can perform literally hundreds of tasks. In this book, you'll learn how to use a router to straight-edge and surface boards; cut dadoes, rabbets, and grooves; work circles and curved surfaces; and create decorative joints. Specialty bits, covered in Chapter 6, will allow a router to do things beyond your wildest dreams.

Routers continue to be viable and expanding tools. Manufacturers are constantly expanding their offerings, providing more power choices and features. Along the same

lines, bit manufacturers employ teams of engineers to design new and innovative cutters to aid in more and more specialized chores. And both manufacturers and woodworkers keep coming up with new accessories and jigs to extend the tool's usefulness and make it safer.

Routers aren't exactly the type of tool you take out of the box, plug in, and handle casually. It takes a bit of practice to develop your skills in using the tool, and a bit of knowledge to transform its capabilities into practical and acceptable applications. To master the router, you should first become a student of it, and use the information on the following pages as your guide.

1

Router Basics

*I*f you're a beginner and you think you're ready to jump right in and start routing wood, you'd better put the brakes on. It's a good idea to get a grasp on a few general techniques before hitting the "on" switch. Once you're armed with some basic knowledge and familiar with some safety precautions, you'll get impressive results—even your first time out.

This chapter will provide you with a general overview of information and techniques you'll need before being introduced to the dozens of more advanced router operations throughout the rest of this book.

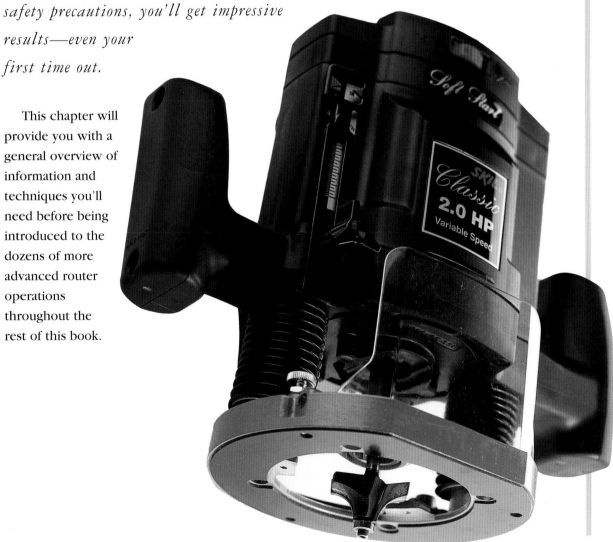

BASIC OPERATION

Your router can be used for many things, from creating decorative edging on wood-work to creating joints for cabinetry. Learn the following basics and you'll be well on your way to becoming a skilled router operator.

The importance of remembering router direction

Remember, a router bit revolves—and *fast*! Always make sure you move the bit in the direction that feeds the stock into its rotation. By doing this, the thrust created by the rotational momentum pulls the bit into the work-piece and forces the router against the straight edge. (In Chapter Two, you'll see a special technique called climb-cutting that works just the opposite.)

Handheld router: When work-ing on *outer* edges, the bit turns clockwise as you look down, so feed the router from left to right (see *below left*). This method also applies to round and curved parts.

When working *inside* edges with a handheld router, you will also feed left to right (see *below left*).

Table-mounted router: The bit rotates counterclockwise, so always feed the workpiece from right to left along the fence with the workpiece in front of the bit and fence. For safety reasons, never feed a workpiece between the bit and the fence.

To make a handheld cut, first secure the workpiece to the bench. Begin with the router in position, but with the bit away from the workpiece. Grip the router, switch on the power, and then slowly slide the router until the bit contacts the work. Once you have full contact between the bit and workpiece, proceed routing, using a smooth, steady feed.

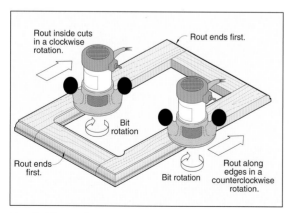

Handheld operation

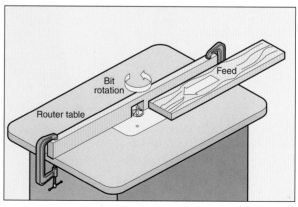

Router-table operation

To minimize splintering, make cuts across the grain first, then the cuts with the grain. If making cross-grain cuts only, back up the workpiece where the bit exits.

Finding the optimum feed rate

Feed rate (not to be confused with router bit speed) refers to the speed at which you move the router along the workpiece or, on a table, the workpiece along a spinning bit. The optimum feed rate will vary, depending on the kind of wood being worked, the router's power, the size and type of bit, and the depth and width of the desired cut.

To figure the proper feed rate, listen to the router, watch the chips and sawdust, and check the finish on the workpiece. At the proper feed rate, the motor should sound like its working under some load but not bogging down. Also, a proper feed rate will produce thin shavings of uniform size.

One indication of forced feeding may be when the usual high-pitched sound changes to a lower, slower sound. Forced feeding often causes excessive wood splintering ahead of the bit or scalloped milling marks on the workpiece edge.

Two common signs that you may be feeding the router too slow are a high-pitch runaway motor sound, and very fine sawdust rather than nice shavings.

Making straight-line cuts with a handheld router

Router cuts that extend from one edge of a workpiece to the other are called *through cuts*. A *stopped cut* extends from one edge but stops short of the other. A *blind cut* stops short of both edges.

Straight-line cuts, such as grooves, dadoes, chamfers, rabbets, mortises, and cut-offs, require a device to guide the router. Use a guide to follow along one edge of the workpiece, or guide the router with a separate straightedge clamped to the workpiece. The following tools can be used in making straightline cuts:

A **straightedge,** such as a straight piece of wood clamped into place or a length of metal clamped across the workpiece so the edge of the router base can slide freely along it, will work well. Typically, you should clamp the straightedge and the workpiece to your bench, offsetting the straightedge enough to locate the cut. The straightedge must be parallel to the workpiece edge.

You can upgrade a basic straightedge by attaching a short piece across one end of it at 90° to make a T-square. Because it's already square, a T-square requires very little time to set up. Just put it into position, clamp, and you're in business.

Piloted bits guide the router along the edge of a workpiece or pattern, whether it's curved or straight. There's a ball bearing or bushing on the end of the bit, so your workpiece must be thick enough to accept the cutter and bearing at the same time.

Scrapwood clamped to the workpiece serves as a straightedge guide for the router to follow. This router's base plate has one flat edge to help guide it.

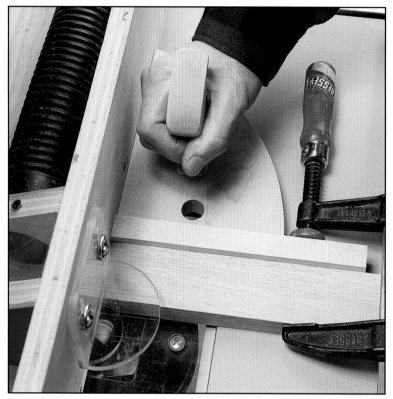

A shop-built pushblock helps move the workpiece past the cutter to rout end grain and minimize chipping. Clamping the workpiece to a pushblock keeps it square to the fence.

The bearing keeps the cut width consistent. It also duplicates the surface it rides against, so the edge must be smooth to avoid transferring imperfections into the cut edge. Be aware that when edge-forming with a piloted bit, less than half of the router base will be supported (at the corners, even less).

Edge guides are often included when you buy a router, but they are also sold separately. Mount one to the router base, then set its edge so the gap between the bit and the guide is equal to the desired spacing.

You can make a *box guide* by fastening two straightedges together between two crosspieces. Space the straightedges so your router slides freely between them but without any slop or excess movement.

Box guides work very well for routing on flat surfaces. Just clamp the box in place and use both hands to move the router. Gluing sandpaper to the underside of the guide will help keep it in place.

Auxiliary *subbases* can be made in any shape or size you want. They're very simple to make—any ¼"- or ⅜"-thick material, such as tempered hardboard or plastic, will do. Use the router's subbase as a pattern to lay out the mounting holes.

How to rout on the contour

The devices you'll need to rout contours are fairly simple to find. Again, piloted bits use bearings to guide the router along a contoured edge. Varying radii can be achieved by using bearings of different diameters. Some edge-forming bits do not have bearings, but you can buy and attach them to the shank above the cutter (similar to pattern bits).

Template guide bushings look like hollow tubes that fit into the center hole of most subbases and guide a router around a template or pattern. During use, the bit extends through the inside of the bushing and beyond the bottom of the router base. When routing, hold the guide bushing against the pattern edge.

Edge guides, which are usually included with new routers, work well in straight-line routing, but some of them can be converted to follow contoured edges too. If your guide has curved edges or a radius guide, use them. If the guide has only a straightedge, you can make your own radius guide for it—simply cut an arc of the same radius as the one you want to follow into one edge of a wooden block. Then, attach this block to the guide's straightedge.

How to cut circles with a router

To cut circles, rotate the router around a pivot point using a circle jig or trammel. A trammel serves as an extended subbase with a pivot point offset from the router bit to the desired radius. The farther the bit is from the pivot point, the larger the circle will be. Trammels can be made infinitely variable so they'll cut circles of almost any diameter. Circle jigs are widely available for purchase. For more tips on routing circles, turn to *page 60*.

Making rabbet cuts with a bit

A rabbeting bit can make rabbet joints and cut rabbets to hold panels of wood or glass or make room for back panels in cabinets. In fact, they can create curved rabbets—unlike your tablesaw or jointer!

To cut rabbets with a handheld router, mount a bearing of the proper diameter to allow the bit to cut to the desired width. Then, set the bit to cutting depth. If the cut

exceeds ¼" square, make multiple shallow cutting passes to reach final depth.

Typical rabbeting bits come with either a 1¼"-diameter cutter and a ½" bearing for cutting ⅜"-deep rabbets, or a 1⅜"-diameter cutter and a ⅜" bearing for cutting ½"-deep rabbets.

You can expand the versatility of a rabbeting bit with a matched set of high-speed bearings like the one shown at *upper right*. Also, see the chart *below*. For more on rabbeting, see *page 19*.

Joint a board with a handheld router

To joint an uneven edge on a board, clamp a straightedge to the top of the piece so it aligns with the edge of the workpiece and rout the edge with a ½" straight bit. (You will need to move the guide back to the distance from the inside edge of the subbase plus ¹⁄₁₆". This way, a straight bit can evenly joint the edge). If the board's edge is so uneven that the cut width exceeds ⅛" in some areas, saw away most of the waste first.

Interchangeable bearings of varying diameters control the cutting width of rabbeting bits.

Working with patterns and templates

To rout a pattern using a handheld router and pattern bit, secure the pattern on top of the workpiece. On a router table, the template goes under the workpiece. When using a plunge router, position the router over the area to be routed and plunge the bit into the field. With a fixed-base router, either bore start-holes in each section to start the bit in, or tip the router and ease the bit into the cut.

Patterns can be made from a variety of materials—tempered hardboard and thick plastic work well. Remember, the template must be thick enough so that the guide bushing can fit against it without bottoming out on the workpiece. For examples of template patterns, see the appendix starting on *page 171*.

Cutting wood joints

Furniture-type joints, such as tongue-and-groove, splined edge, mortise and tenon, half-lap and cross-lap, dovetail

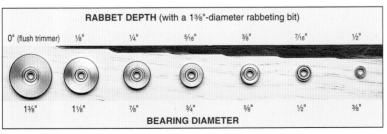

RABBET DEPTH (with a 1⅜"-diameter rabbeting bit)

0" (flush trimmer)	⅛"	¼"	⁵⁄₁₆"	⅜"	⁷⁄₁₆"	½"
1⅜"	1⅛"	⅞"	¾"	⅝"	½"	⅜"

BEARING DIAMETER

Samples of cutting depths made by different rabbeting bits and bearing combinations.

dado, and the numerous variations of the rabbet and dado can all be cut with a router.

Many jigs are available to help cut joint parts. Many of them position the stock so the bit can be centered accurately and repeatedly. A few can be used to cut the parts. You can make many of these jigs and fixtures yourself.

Turn your router into a stationary machine

By mounting your handheld router in a table, you will turn it into a stationary machine, but one that can perform many additional tasks. Tables tend to provide more control over the cutting operation. There are plenty of readily available, commercial options, from small bench-top tables to solid, floor-standing models. But, if you'd like to build your own, you'll find plans and instructions for making three types of router tables in Chapter 3. In Chapter 4, you'll read about ways to get

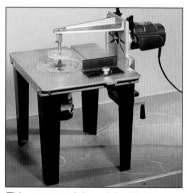
This commercial model table is good for cutting, jointing, and edge-forming.

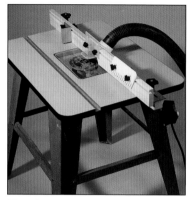
The fence acts as a permanent straightedge on a router table.

the most out of your table-mounted router.

On a router table, the **fence** serves as the straightedge. The bit and fence remain stationary, so you move the workpiece along the fence. Again, for safety reasons, never feed a workpiece between the fence and the spinning bit.

Cuts on the router table

All types of grooved cuts, whether dadoes, grooves, rabbets, or sliding dovetails, can be made on a router table. For most jobs, use a bit the same diameter as the width of the groove you want to cut. If you need a groove that's not a standard bit size, make two passes with a slightly smaller bit to get the width needed, moving the fence for the second pass.

To cut rabbets on a table, first elevate the bit to cutting depth, then position the fence to establish cut width. If the rabbet's width exceeds the bit's

diameter, adjust the fence to make additional cutting passes.

For other grooved cuts, many woodworkers prefer to use up-cutting spiral bits, because when they are inverted under a table, they pull the chips and dust down and out of the cut. Also, feed the workpiece with the crown of the end-grain rings pointing down whenever possible, and use feather boards or holddowns to hold the workpiece against the fence and flat on the table.

Routing *stopped cuts* (see *page 36*) gets a bit more tricky on a router table because the cut is made on the underside of the workpiece, where you can't see it. To make a half-blind cut, first mark your cutting line on the face or outside edge of the workpiece, where it will be visible to you. Next, using a small square, mark the bit's cutting edge on the fence or on the table. (A piece of masking tape on the table's face will suffice.) Then, start the router, move the workpiece into the bit, and stop the cut when the line on the work aligns with the bit mark.

To make a full-blind cut on a table, follow the same procedure, but mark the bit's diameter on the fence or table and both stop and start lines on the workpiece. Then, turn on the router and place the work against the fence with the left end suspended and its right end resting on the router table. Slowly lower the workpiece completely onto the bit with the left mark about ½" to the left of the bit. Feed the workpiece to the right until the left mark on the fence and workpiece align. Now, feed the workpiece from right to left until right marks on the stock and fence align.

Using stops for cutting multiple pieces

To blind-rout multiple pieces quickly and accurately, clamp stops to the router table fence. Lay out the cut on the workpiece, then measure from the left end of the cut to the right end of the piece. Using this measurement, locate the *right* stop by measuring to the right from the left edge of the router bit.

To set the *left* stop, measure from the right end of the cut to the left end of the workpiece. Use this measurement starting from the right edge of the router bit. Clamp the stops in place, position the piece against the right stop, turn on the router, drop the workpiece on the spinning center, and then feed the piece to the left until it touches the left stop.

Jointing on a router table

If your table has a split fence, first align both fence sections with the front edge of the bit. Then, move the outfeed side of the fence forward—the same thickness of the material you want to remove (typically ¹⁄₁₆") when jointing a board edge. Lock the section in place. Feed the piece right to

left and apply pressure against the outfeed side of the fence.

Jointing a board on a router table with a one-piece fence requires one fence modification. You must use glue, cement, or double-faced tape to secure a piece of thin material, such as a ¹⁄₁₆"-thick piece of plastic laminate, to the outfeed portion of the fence. This will provide the necessary offset. Next, position the outfeed table so its face aligns tangent to the outside cutting edge of the bit. *Note: this will leave the infeed end of the fence offset at a distance equal to the thickness of the laminate and tape. Then, holding the workpiece against the fence, feed it from right to left.*

Edge-forming

You can edge-form round or contoured pieces on a router table without a fence, but this requires a piloted bit and a start pin or starting block to serve as a pivot point for the workpiece. To do this, first position the workpiece against the start pin or block, then slowly rotate it into the cutter until it contacts the bearing. Feed the piece

against the bit's rotation. Draw it away from the bit when done.

The start pin should be inserted into the table top an inch or two from the bit. You can also clamp a start block in about the same position on the table. Always clamp a guard over the bit so you can't get your fingers near the cutting edges.

From round-over bit to beading bit

To cut a standard round-over, adjust the bit so that the bottom of the concave cutting edge aligns flush with the router base (handheld) or the surface of the router table. Use a flat block of wood to check the setting. Next, test the setting on scrap stock. Adjust the bit until you are satisfied with the cut, then rout your workpieces.

> *Tip: You can add a touch of class to a round-over profile by setting up the same bit to cut a fillet. Raise the bit above the table to set the desired depth of the fillet.*

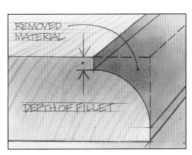

By extending a round-over bit, you can form an edge with an interesting, decorative fillet like this.

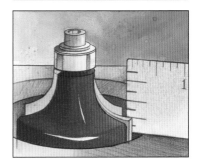

It's best to use a ruler when setting the bit for cutting fillet depth precisely.

A FEW HELPFUL TIPS

While you are familiarizing yourself with your router, these four tips will come in handy in getting you the best results quickly and safely.

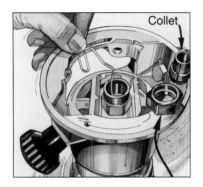

Collet

1 Before getting started, always inspect the collet assembly for resin, wood dust, and other debris that can make bit removal difficult. To avoid sticky situations, start by removing the collet locking nut and collet. Then, blow away any loose debris with an air-hose. With a paper clip, gently scrape any gunk that remains, as shown *above.* (We removed the router subbase for clarity.) Soften stubborn resins with lacquer thinner, then wipe clean. ***Note:*** *Always unplug the router when servicing the collet assembly or changing to a different bit.*

2 Another culprit that can make bit removal a hassle is burrs on the bit

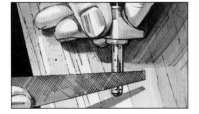

shank. Remove them with a few light file strokes, as shown at *bottom left.* Now, securely lock the bit into the collet.

3 For the best possible cut, move the router along the edges of the surface in a counterclockwise direction. When routing all four edges, cut the end-grain edges first, then cut the edge-grain lengths to minimize edge-grain splinters.

Move the router at a consistent speed, and increase the feed rate if burning occurs. If the grain tears out, take several light passes.

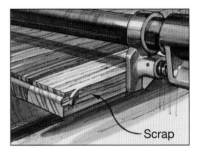

Scrap

4 When routing end grain, it's a good idea to back the existing (last) end-grain cut with scrap to prevent splintering of the workpiece. *Above*, a bit chipped out the scrap block but left the corner of the workpiece crisp and clean.

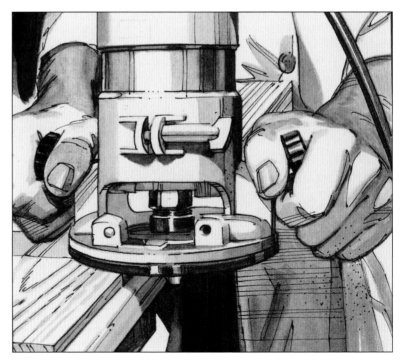

ROUTER SAFETY

A router's high speed and considerable torque can result in loss of control that can quickly ruin a workpiece and result in injury. To help you get full enjoyment from your woodworking—and peace of mind while using your router—here's some sound safety advice compiled from woodworking professionals.

Router fashion tips

Inside your shop, what you wear can directly contribute to your safety. So dress comfortably, but follow the rules.

■ Always wear safety goggles, safety glasses with side shields, or a full-face shield. (Even with this protection, always keep your face and eyes away from a spinning bit.)

■ It's important to wear hearing protection, even for short periods of router use. A router's screech can permanently damage your ears. OSHA noise level charts indicate that a 105-dB level (a special decibel measurement for noise) results in some hearing loss after even only one hour's exposure. Routers typically produce from 105–110 dB, and they can really wail when a bit starts to dull! The type of protection you choose must therefore have a high enough noise-reduction rating (NRR) to lower the router's ruckus to a safer plateau. So you'll need hearing protection with at least a 20 dB NRR to reduce the sound to an acceptable 90 dB. (Hearing protection, from plugs to muffs, usually include their NRR information on the packaging.)

■ Never wear gloves, loose clothing, jewelry, or dangling objects (even hair) that may catch in rotating parts or accessories.

Proceed with caution

Your router may seem like a snap to operate, but looks can be deceiving. So, before you begin cutting, make sure to familiarize yourself with the parts of your router as diagrammed in the owner's manual. In addition, always follow these precautions:

■ Be sure that your router is unplugged—not just turned off—when you change bits or set the depth of a cut. Always clear your worktable or router table of all tools and debris.

■ Follow the tool manufacturer's recommended procedures for setting your router's depth of cut, and be sure to tighten all adjustment locks.

■ Use the wrenches provided with your router to install router bits, and carefully read the owner's manual regarding the proper method of doing so.

■ Be sure that the cutter shaft is properly engaged in the collet. Usually, that means bottoming out the bit in the collet, then raising it $\frac{1}{16}$". An improperly installed bit can come out and be propelled at great speed in any direction.

■ Flick the switch to the "off" position when plugging the router into the electrical outlet as well as when you disconnect it.

Careful with that router, Eugene!

There isn't a power tool that compares with a router's versatility when it's used properly. However, there are few tools that can surprise you more. So, like a scout, always be prepared!

■ Secure all clamping devices on your workpiece—as well as those that hold your workpiece—before doing any freehand routing. Likewise, firmly secure all fences and jigs before routing on a router table.

■ If you use your router mounted in a router table, make sure the tool is fastened into place *tightly*, with safety guards in position and a pushstick and/or pushblock close at hand.

■ Always check to make certain that the router's clockwise rotation is cutting with the grain of the wood, or like a car that suddenly gains traction in the mud, it can leap. This will help you remember: In freehand routing, when you hold the router in front of you on the stock, it should always move from *left to right.* On a router table, because the tool is inverted and the stock is directly in your hands, you move the stock from *right to left.* Paint a feed-direction arrow on your router table as a direction reminder.

■ Keep your hands away from the cutter area when you plug the router in and turn it on.

■ Because of the torque a router produces, keep a firm grasp with both hands *only* on the handles and gripping surfaces provided by the tool's manufacturer.

■ On some types of cuts, table-mounted routers can pull your fingers into the bit. The drawings *below* show you two safe setups that avoid this possibility.

■ If possible, always turn the cutter opening on the router away from your body while routing. If your router has a chip shield over the opening, see that it is properly and securely installed.

■ Never use a dull bit. It adds to the router's workload and can burn the wood. If pushed, it may break and fly off, causing injury.

■ For greatest control, allow the router to reach full speed before feeding it into the wood. Never begin routing with the bit in place against the wood, and never force a router into the wood when you're making a shaping cut.

■ Never attempt to remove debris from a spinning router bit with your fingers.

■ Keep the base of the router and its whirling cutter bit away from you when removing it from the workpiece. Let it come to a full stop before setting it down, and then always lay the router on its side, clear of any clutter.

■ Let the bit and collet cool down after routing, and before making any changes.

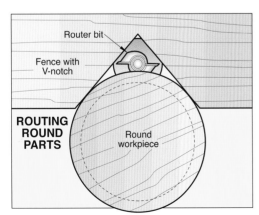

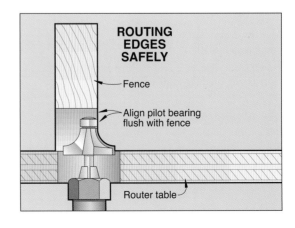

SPECIAL FEATURE: ROUTER MAINTENANCE

The following maintenance procedures will help ensure safe routing:

1 Keep all mating areas of your router free of dust, resin, pitch accumulation, and grit. Resin-filled dust particles can get through slits in the collet, become impacted, and adversely effect the bit shanks, collet, threads, and spindle. It's a good idea to periodically remove and disassemble all parts of the collet and give them a thorough cleaning with solvents or pitch remover. The only way to loosen or remove dust particles is with a hard-pointed object such as a scratch awl, but when using one, be careful not to scratch any part of the smooth contact surfaces of the collet or damage any interior threads.

2 If you feel any unusual vibrations in the router, check the bit first—it may be bent, chipped, or running off-center. It also may be improperly ground, without adequate relief clearance, be carrying an excessive chip load due to an excessive feed rate, or simply be the wrong bit design for the job.

3 Check your bearings frequently. Routers tend to place a lot of strain on their bearings, so replace any that are showing signs of deterioration immedi-

ately. If you do notice vibration and think it might be the bearings, disconnect the power and remove the collet and collet lock nut. Turn the motor shaft (spindle) slowly, feeling for rough or irregular rotation. Try pushing the spindle from side to side and then up and down to detect any movement. There should not be any movement at all. If there is, it's quite likely that the ball bearings are rough and in need of replacing.

4 Check the collet. Collets do wear, particularly if they're made from lower-grade steel. To determine if yours will wear, rub a file against it. If it can make a cut against your collet, your collet isn't tempered, and it might be subject to premature wear. Vibrations can indicate collet wear, which in turn causes bit run-out (when the bit is not running or rotating on its central axis). Get into the habit of inspecting bit shanks as you remove them from the collet. Markings on the shank usually indicate that the collet may be worn.

5 Clean the mating parts between the metal and the motor housing of fixed-base routers. Friction and stickiness can develop in these

areas and affect your routing. Just apply a paste wax or dry lubricant to keep them running smoothly. Also, clean and lubricate the posts of plunge routers on a regular basis with dry lubricant or silicone spray.

6 Blow the dust out from the motor, switch housings, and other areas where it might accumulate. From time to time, tighten all screws, and if necessary, replace worn motor brushes, frayed electrical cords, plugs, and switches.

SHOP TIP

These two maintenance tips will save wear and tear on your router:

- Slip a length of vinyl hose over the handles of collet wrenches so they don't hit and dent the plunging posts as you are changing bits.

- Apply a coat of paste wax to the router subbase for smoother feeding with less effort.

2

Router Techniques

Working with a router is a bit like higher education—the more you learn, the more there is to learn. And while it's true that experience is always the best teacher, you'll be off to a good start in routing techniques after reading this chapter. In the following pages you'll learn tips to improve routing skills you may already have, but will probably learn a thing or two you never even thought about. Some of the techniques discussed apply solely to handheld routers; others to table-mounted routers. (See Chapter Four for more table-specific techniques.)

This chapter contains just a few of the multitude of projects and designs that are possible with your router. The techniques described here are by no means an exhaustive list of all the work you can accomplish with this versatile tool. But, on the following pages, you'll see a great sampling of techniques that you can learn and apply to other projects that you dream up as your experience grows.

While the cuts you will use in routing are practically infinite, they normally fall into one of two categories. **Edge routing** includes those cuts that are made, as the name implies, on the edges of a workpiece. These may be decorative, such as round-over or cove cuts, or purely functional, as with a rabbet. The other common category is **field routing**. This type of routing cut is made inside the edges of a workpiece. These too can be decorative, as when using a V-groove bit for lettering a sign, or functional, such as employing a straight bit to do a dado.

With these two categories of router cuts in mind, you'll discover that cuts of either type may be employed in joining two pieces of wood together for furniture and cabinetry, preparing wood for further machining, or decorating one or all of the surfaces on a workpiece. Read on for techniques that utilize one or the other, or both.

On the following pages you'll learn some solid "cornerstone" techniques of routing, such as rabbeting, decorative and practical joinery, edging panels, routing stopped cuts, routing raised panel doors, and even creating a scooped-out chair seat. You'll also pick up a number of expert "Shop tips" along the way, so with a bit of time and a little elbow grease, you'll be well on the way toward honing your router expertise!

TWO WAYS OF RABBETING

A rabbet is simply a rectangular recess along the edge or end of a workpiece, as shown in the illustration here. Most often used as joints in casework, rabbets are also sometimes used as design features in molding, recesses to hold artwork in frames, or as half-lap or shiplap joints.

RABBET DEPTH

A TYPICAL RABBET JOINT

RABBET WIDTH

Although simple in appearance, there's more to the rabbet cut than meets the eye. To make best use of rabbets, you should know the following two ways to cut them, when to use each method, and how to make the cuts effectively.

1 Handheld router with a rabbeting bit

Unlike saw blades and dado sets, router bits do not leave tiny scoring marks. So, use a router bit if the surface or ends of the rabbets will be visible in your finished project.

If you need to rabbet an opening inside a surface rather than along an outside edge or end, using a router bit is your only option. Some such instances would include a router-table opening for receiving a router insert plate, or the inside of an assembled door frame for accepting a piece of glass.

With a handheld router, you typically use a rabbeting bit with a pilot bearing, as shown *above*. This way, you can change the cut width simply by changing bearings. You can even cut rabbets along curved edges.

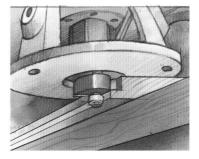

2 Router table with a straight bit

Although it's not always easy to rabbet large pieces on a router table, this method has some distinct advantages over using a handheld router. First, a router table has a fence that ensures a perfectly straight rabbet (a bearing-piloted bit will follow any irregularities in the work-piece edge). And, although a piloted rabbeting bit will help you cut a rabbet up to ½" wide and ½" deep, you can put a large straight bit in the router table to cut rabbets up to 1 × 1" or wider.

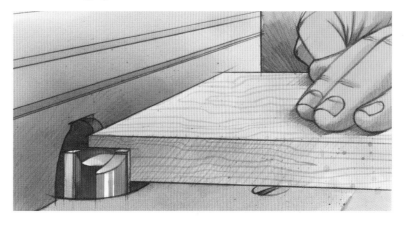

DECORATIVE JOINT REINFORCEMENTS

If you're thinking, "Boy, those joints sure look great—I wish I could do that," you're in for a pleasant surprise. Armed with the information in this section (and a little practice) you will be able to produce equally impressive results fairly quickly. So if you're ready to take your project-building skills to a new, higher level (and amaze your family and friends with your special talent), read on. We'll have you up and running in no time flat.

Although tight-fitting miters are a source of much pride for woodworkers, the bad news is that these plain-looking joints rank low on the list of strongest joints. The good news is that you can beautify miters and make them much stronger in one fell swoop. The answer: *corner keys*.

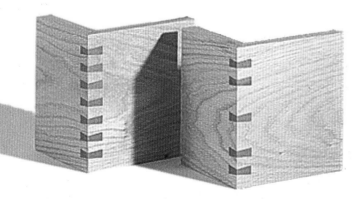

These consist of small pieces of wood in various shapes that fit tightly into slots (called *key ways*) cut diagonally through the miter joint. Viewed from either side of the joint, corner keys of different shapes give the appearance of dovetail, box, or finger joints. In this section, we'll show you how to make a variety of corner keys useful for projects ranging from jewelry boxes to hope chests.

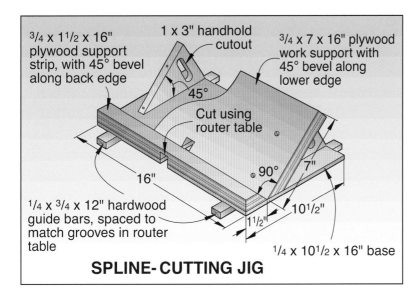

3/4 x 1 1/2 x 16" plywood support strip, with 45° bevel along back edge

1 x 3" handhold cutout

3/4 x 7 x 16" plywood work support with 45° bevel along lower edge

45°

Cut using router table

90°   7"

16"

1/4 x 3/4 x 12" hardwood guide bars, spaced to match grooves in router table

1 1/2"   10 1/2"

1/4 x 10 1/2 x 16" base

SPLINE-CUTTING JIG

First, you'll need a simple jig and a few router bits

In order to cut the key ways, you will need to build the spline-cutting jig shown *above*. This handy device holds a mitered corner at a 45° angle as you pass the joint through a router bit. Building one requires only a few scraps of wood and about an hour of your time. It should be at least twice as wide as your longest miter joint. (The shop-made version pictured here handles miters up to 8" long.)

Unless your router table already has twin miter-gauge slots, you'll need to add these so they can accept the guide strips on the underside of the jig. You also can modify your router table by clamping a board (of the necessary width) to it and routing the slots, as shown in **Photo A**.

Make sure the board you use as the straightedge has two perfectly parallel edges. Cut the guide strips so they fit the slots snugly, and attach the strips after cutting the slots. Apply paraffin wax to the strips and slots so the jig glides smoothly.

You can make various keyed joints using either dovetail, round nose, or straight router bits. The examples on the following page with keys within keys will require two router bits, one about 1/4" to 3/8" smaller in diameter than the other. If you decide to make a dovetail within a dovetail, the bits should have the same cutting angle. (Dovetail bits vary from 7° to 14° in cutting angle. There are 8° bits of 3/4" and 3/8" diameters in the workpieces shown in this project.)

If your router table doesn't have two parallel slots, rout them for receiving the spline-cutting jig.

Take a minute to do some simple planning

You can space the keys evenly or unevenly, but in either case you will need to determine their center-to-center spacing, as shown in the drawing below. The height of the keys should be equal to the thickness of your workpieces.

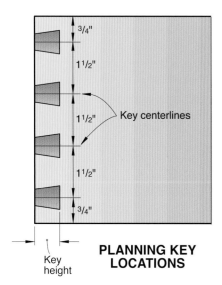

PLANNING KEY LOCATIONS

Put the jig into action

Using the center-to-center spacings, cut blocks of wood in widths that match your spacings. In the example shown *above*, there are three identical blocks, each cut 1½" wide. (You don't need blocks for the edge-to-center spacings.) The blocks should be just as thick as your workpieces and between 4 and 6" long. You should chamfer all block edges slightly to help ensure that debris does not

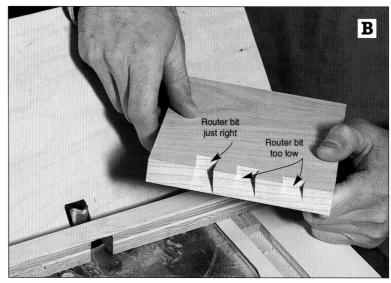

Adjust the router bit to cut through the thickness of the workpiece and no more.

prevent them from solidly contacting each other. Number the blocks and set them aside.

Now, with a scrap piece of the same thickness as your workpieces, determine the correct router-bit height. Do this by making test cuts like those shown in **Photo B**. The bit should cut across the full width of the workpiece edge, but no more.

Position a stopblock to make your first router cut of an end key.

To make other cuts, add spacer blocks as wide as the center-to-center spacing of your keys.

■ To make *dovetail keys,* use an adjustable triangle to set your tablesaw blade to the same angle as the router bit's cutting edge. Rip one edge of your key stock at this angle, then readjust the fence and cut the tapered key, as shown in **Photo E.**

Be sure to set the blade angle accurately before ripping the key stock as shown.

On your workpiece (a mitered box in this case), mark the center of either end key. Align this mark with the center of the router bit and clamp a stopblock onto the jig, as shown in **Photo C.** Measure the position of the cut, and readjust the stopblock if necessary. Mark an "X" on the end of your box that goes against the stopblock. Clamp your box to the jig.

After making the first cut, rotate the box to make the same cut in each mitered corner. Add one of the spacer blocks and repeat the cutting procedure. Continue this way until you cut slots for all of the keys, as shown in **Photo D.**

How to make your keys

Making keys for box and finger joints is relatively simple—just cut rectangular pieces of a contrasting wood that fit snugly into the slots. However, dovetail and rounded-finger keys require some extra effort. Here's some advice for each type:

■ Like finger and box keys, *rounded-finger keys* require that you cut rectangular pieces of wood that fit exactly into the slots. Then, round over both corners of one edge with a round-over bit. (Use a fence to make the second round-over cut.) The radius of the round-over bit should match the radius of the round-nose bit used to cut the slot.

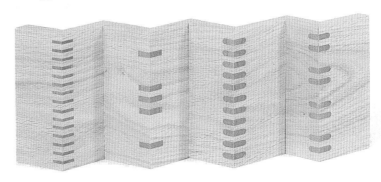

Install the keys

Cut the key stock to lengths just longer than the key slots, apply glue to the mating surfaces, and gently tap them into the slots. After the glue dries, saw off as much of the key stock as possible without marring the surrounding surfaces. **Photo F** shows this being done with a protective piece of cardboard and a Japanese-style handsaw. Other saws will work, but be careful not to damage the surrounding wood surfaces. Finally, remove the excess key stock with a stationary belt sander.

A piece of cardboard will protect your workpieces as you cut away excess key stock.

How to make key-within-key reinforcements

It's easy to place one key within another. First, install keys in all of the corners of your project as already described. Then, make an extra corner from scrapwood that also has the first keys already in place. Next, install a smaller router bit and adjust its height by making test cuts in the scrap piece, as shown in the photo at *right*. Cut the slots by using the same stopblock and spacer blocks in the same order used to cut the larger key slots. Once you're satisfied with the results, repeat the steps for the second dovetail cuts in your actual project.

Working with scrap stock, adjust the height of the cut for the second key, as shown here.

DRESS UP YOUR PROJECTS WITH BOW TIES

Like keys, surface splines in the shape of bow ties can add both strength and style to butted surfaces. You can add them to mitered frame corners or to panels, such as the example at **bottom right.** *The following will teach you how to add such a spline to a mitered frame corner.*

What you'll need

It's preferable to use a plunge router for this procedure, but most any router will get the job done. (For more on the plunge router, see *page 47.*) You'll also need a ½"-outside-diameter guide bushing for the base of your router, ¼"- and ⅛"-diameter straight bits, and two 8 × 10" pieces of ⅜" or ½" plywood.

In addition, you'll need a pattern for cutting the spline template—three choices are provided in the appendix on *page 171.* The shaded portions of these patterns show the finished size of the bow tie.

First, make your templates

Create the spline template from one of the pieces of plywood. In its center, cut a hole in the shape of one of the spline templates. A scroll saw works best for this. Mark "spline" on this template.

To make the mortise template, mount a ½" O.D. guide bushing and ¼" straight bit into your router. Then, clamp the spline template, your other piece of plywood, and two pieces of scrap wood to your bench, as shown in **Photo A.**

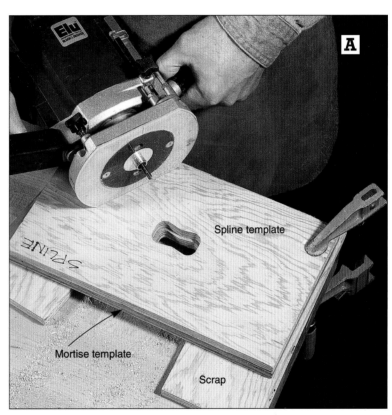

Use the spline template to cut the mortise template.

Using the spline template as a guide, cut completely through the mortise template. (The scrap keeps the bit away from your bench.)

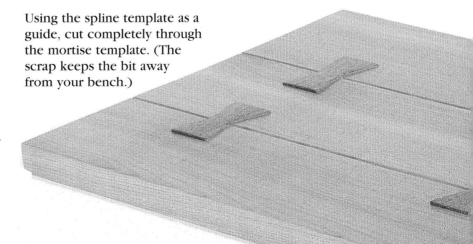

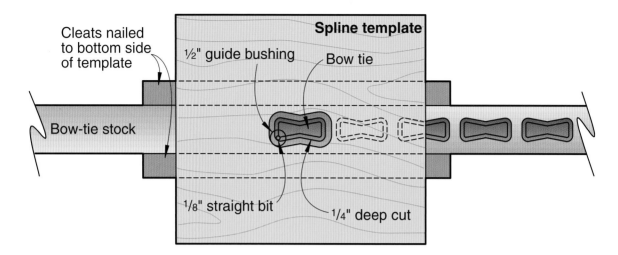

Cut the bow ties

Replace the ¼" straight bit with an ⅛" straight bit. Then, nail two cleats of the same thickness as your bow-tie stock to the bottom side of the spline template, spaced by the width of the work-piece, as shown in the drawing *above*.

Set the straight bit for a ¼"-deep cut, and clamp the spline template and bow-tie stock to your workbench, as shown in **Photo B.** Finally, moving the router in a clockwise motion, with the guide bushing against the spline-template wall, cut the decorative bow ties to shape.

Adjust your tablesaw fence for cutting ¼"-thick bow ties on the outboard side of the blade (the side opposite the fence). Cut the splines, as shown in **Photo C.**

How to install your splines

Visually center a bow tie on the joint of your project, and trace its outline with a pencil. Center this outline inside the hole in the mortise template,

Keep the guide bushing firmly against the wall of the spline template to cut well-shaped bow ties.

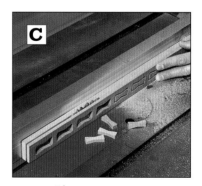

Cut the ¼"-thick splines (bow ties) on the outboard side of your table-saw blade.

and clamp the template to the workpiece, as shown in **Photo D.** Turn this assembly upside down, and nail cleats (the same thickness as the workpieces) to the bottom of the template, as shown in **Photo E.**

Turn the template and workpiece rightside up, and clamp these to your workbench. Adjust the ⅛" straight bit for a cut about ¹⁄₁₆" deeper than when it was used to cut the bow ties. Cut the mortise by following the wall of the template hole, and then hog-

ging out the field material until the hole has a flat bottom. Remove the template. Glue the bow-tie spline into the mortise, allow the glue to dry, and sand the splines flush with the surface.

Note: In the case of the splines in the mission-style panel on page 25, the bow ties were left about ¹⁄₁₆" higher than the panel surface. So, the step of sanding was skipped, and the sharp corners were chamfered instead.

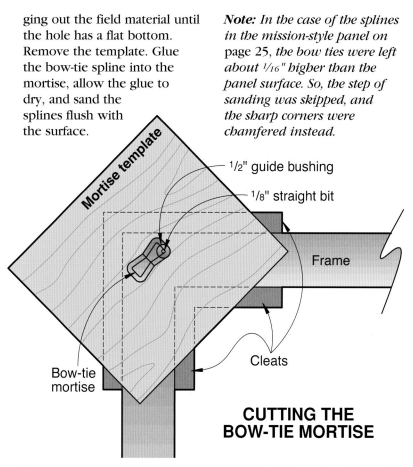

Mortise template

½" guide bushing

⅛" straight bit

Frame

Cleats

Bow-tie mortise

CUTTING THE BOW-TIE MORTISE

Center and clamp the mortise template over the marked outline of the bow tie on your mitered workpiece.

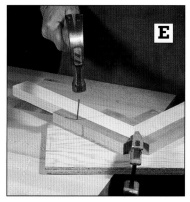

Cleats nailed to the bottom of the mortise template hold the workpiece in position.

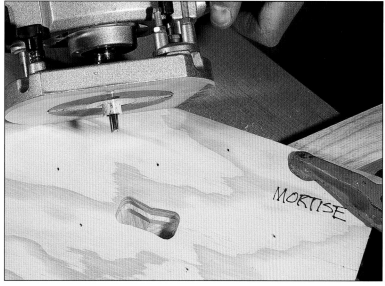

Try to vacuum the debris from the mortise as you rout it to prevent chips from interfering with the cut.

ROUTING A SCOOPED CHAIR SEAT

First appearing more than 250 years ago, Windsor chairs featured seats scooped out of a solid wood plank. Back then, hollowing out the seat was done by hand with an adze and inshave. You could do it that way (many chairmakers still do), but why not take a modern approach and use your router and a jig that is easy to make? Use the pair to make chair seats in the Windsor style, or even one for a rocking chair.

Arrow shows routing direction

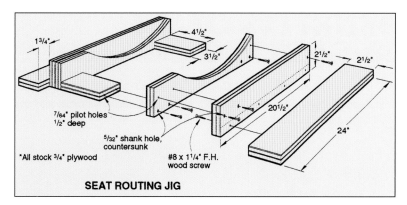

SEAT ROUTING JIG

Build a simple router jig to start

Refer to the Seat Routing Jig drawing, *above,* and the Guide Rail Pattern on *pages 172-173* of this book. Then cut the parts for the routing jig to size.

Note: The pattern on pages 172–173 *is at 75% of full-size. You will need to convert the pattern before you apply it to this project.*

You should temporarily laminate the blanks for the two guide rails (shown in A) with double-faced tape, and apply the converted Guide Rail Pattern to the stack. Bandsaw the curve, taking care to make a smooth, continuous arc. Sand the curved edge, and separate the parts.

Mount a $\frac{1}{4} \times 6 \times 6$" auxiliary base on your router, and install a $\frac{3}{4}$" straight bit. (One with a $\frac{1}{2}$" shank will stand up well to the heavy cutting.) Adjust the bit to extend $1\frac{9}{32}$" below the base.

Clamp the jig to a piece of scrapwood (the photos show a 2' length of 2 × 8), with the arrow pointing to your right.

Then, place the router at the left end of the jig, turn it on, and make a full pass in the direction of the arrow. Turn off the router, and lift it from the jig. The bit will cut a ramp in the spacer block at the left end of the jig. You'll use this sloped slot to align the jig when shaping the seat.

Now, rout the scoop-out

Attach the paper pattern of your chair seat to the seat blank (spray adhesive works best), or sketch it on if you're designing it yourself. Then clamp the seat blank to your workbench.

Place the jig on the blank, aligning the corners of the jig's exit ramp along the solid pattern line on the right side of the seat. (The photo at *right* shows the alignment points at a later stage of the routing.) Slide the jig straight toward the front edge of the blank so about two-thirds of the ramp's width lies over the blank, and clamp it in place. Make sure the clamps don't interfere with router movement in the guide rails.

Then, place the router at the end of the jig that's toward the center of the seat. Turn it on, and slide it along the curve in the guide rails. As you exit the cut, turn off the router; then lift it from the jig. Don't lift the router out of the jig before turning it off, and don't try to go back through the cut in the other direction.

Unclamp the jig, and move it to make the next cut. Again, align the corners of the exit ramp with the pattern line, and position the jig so you'll be cutting with about two-thirds of the bit's width. Start the router, make another pass as before, and shut off the router after the bit exits the work. Periodically recheck the router-bit protrusion distance and ensure that the collet is tight.

Continue moving the jig around the blank counterclockwise, always moving the router in the direction of the arrow, as shown in the opening photo on *page 28.* As a point of reference, it can take up to 75 or so passes to complete.

As you move the jig around the seat, align both corners of the exit ramp along the pattern line as indicated. Place the jig so you cut with about two-thirds of the bit's width.

SPECIAL FEATURE: THE BENEFITS OF CLIMB-CUTTING

Sometimes, it makes sense to go in the opposite direction of prevailing wisdom. Such is the case with climb-cutting—the practice of running a handheld router in a clockwise motion around the edge of a workpiece.

How this procedure gives you smooth routed edges

As shown on the *next page*, when you feed a router in the typical counterclockwise direction, the bit's cutting edges lift the grain of the workpiece. But, in a climb cut, the bit pulls the grain down as its cutting edges enter the workpiece.

So, with a climb-cut you don't get the splintering that you often get with a bit fed counterclockwise. Plus, climb-cutting has a burnishing effect on the wood, leaving an exceptionally smooth routed surface. For these reasons, some woodworkers choose to climb cut most times when they use handheld routers on edges.

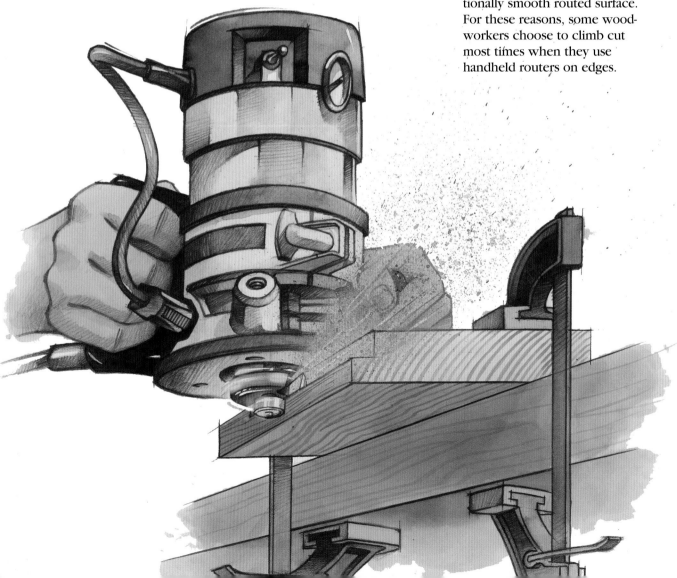

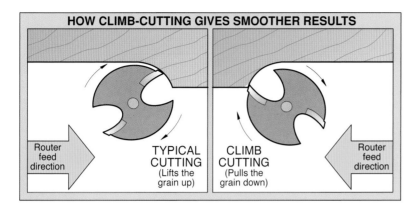

HOW CLIMB-CUTTING GIVES SMOOTHER RESULTS

Router feed direction

TYPICAL CUTTING (Lifts the grain up)

CLIMB CUTTING (Pulls the grain down)

Router feed direction

How to make a climb-cut

Climb-cutting takes a little getting used to, so practice this technique with small router bits and scrap softwood. Remove no more than ⅛" of stock when using small bits, and restrict yourself to about ¹⁄₁₆" of stock removal when using larger bits, such as ½" cove bits. Always use sharp bits, and *never* climb-cut with bits more than 2" in diameter.

When you climb-cut, your router will want to run away from you, so hold on firmly with both hands. The workpiece should be firmly clamped down.

Because a climb-cutting bit does not tend to pull into the workpiece, you don't have to lower your bit to increase its cut for each successive pass. Simply set the bit to its full cutting depth and remove a little more stock with each cut. You'll be surprised how quickly you can rout edges, and how much control you'll have over this "freehand" process (provided you take light cuts).

Although you get little splintering with a climb-cut, it still makes sense to follow the traditional wisdom of routing the ends of a workpiece before routing the edges. If you see some "fuzzing" of the grain when you climb-cut, you probably have a dull bit. (Some woods, such as butternut and willow, will fuzz with even the sharpest bits.)

When *not* to climb-cut

Under many circumstances, it's still best to feed a router in a counterclockwise direction because a bit fed that way tends to "pull" into the workpiece, template, or straightedge that you guide it against. This tendency to "hug" whatever you guide the router against serves you well when it's essential that the router not wander off course. For example, when cutting a dado, or the groove for holding a tambour door in the example at *right*, the cut must follow its guiding edge exactly.

Also, *always* feed a workpiece in the typical right-to-left direction whenever you use a router table. If you try to climb-cut, the bit will pull the workpiece away from you, creating an unsafe situation (not to mention poorquality cuts).

However, if you have the luxury of a power feeder mounted to your router table or shaper, climb-cutting produces silky-smooth moldings with these stationary tools. That's because the power feeder controls the workpiece for a rock-steady cut, and your hands never come close to the cutting edges.

With man-made materials such as Corian or mediumdensity fiberboard (MDF), there's no advantage to climbcutting because these materials have no natural grain that might tear out.

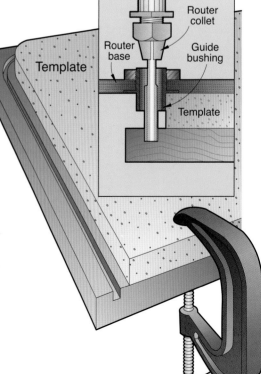

Router collet

Router base

Guide bushing

Template

Template

PUTTING A FINISHED EDGE ON PANELS

When you use plywood in a project, such as a bookcase, it's a good idea to dress up the visible edges. The best way to do this is with solid-wood edging, which usually has to be flush-trimmed to match the plywood's thickness. You can do this with a hand-held router and flush-trimming bit, but chances are good that you'll tip the router and gouge the work. The router-table-mounted fence shown here solves the problem when you have a number of panels or shelves to create.

Made of ¾" plywood, the fence sits perpendicular to the table, as shown *above*. The lower edge of the fence is mounted 1" above the router-table surface, so it can accommodate edging up to ¾" thick.

To build the jig, cut its identically sized fence and base to 11¾" wide. Measure your router table to determine the length. Then cut matching notches in the base and fence, positioned to align with the bit hole in your table. Two triangular braces hold the base and fence together. The cleats at each end help position the assembly on your router table.

To stiffen the entire assembly, add a support panel to the braces. You can cut a hole in the support panel to accommodate a shop-vacuum hose, which comes in handy when collecting chips.

To use the fence, install a flush-trim bit in your table-mounted router. Align the fence face flush with the bit's pilot bearing, and clamp the fence down. Hold the edged plywood firmly against the fence as you make each pass, and the edging should come out perfectly flush every time.

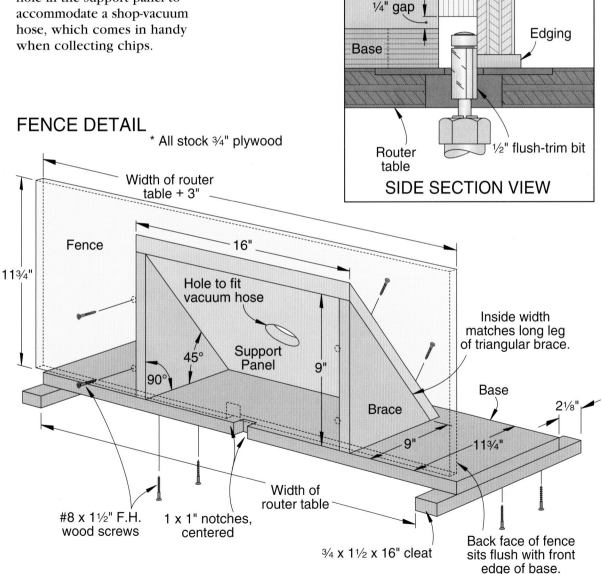

SIDE SECTION VIEW

FENCE DETAIL
* All stock ¾" plywood

SPECIAL FEATURE: AVOIDING ROUTER BURNS

Burns on the edges of a workpiece can lead to a sanding nightmare or much worse—they actually can ruin a project altogether. But armed with the right measures, you shouldn't have to worry about burns at all. Here are five tips:

1 Buy router bits with ball-bearing pilots.

Although router bits with ball-bearing pilots cost a few dollars more, you'll find the extra investment well worth it. Bearingless pilots heat up as they spin against the edge of a workpiece. Pilots with bearings run cooler because the tip of the router bit spins on the inside of the lubricated bearing, while the outside of the bearing coolly rolls along the workpiece.

2 Keep those bits sharp.

Dull cutting edges—another source of friction—can burn a workpiece by rubbing the wood rather than cleanly shearing it. The solutions: 1) Buy carbide-tipped bits—they stay sharp longer than steel bits; and 2) have your router bits sharpened at the first signs of dulling. Sharpening shops usually charge between $4 and $7 for sharpening bits less than 1" in diameter.

3 Make light, multiple cuts.

Even a sharp, ball-bearing piloted router bit will burn wood if you feed the router too slowly or stop the machine while the bit is spinning. Remember to keep your router moving at a steady rate (but not so fast that the router sounds labored). To accomplish this, take several light cuts, as shown *below,* instead of one or two heavy ones that may cause you to slow the feed rate.

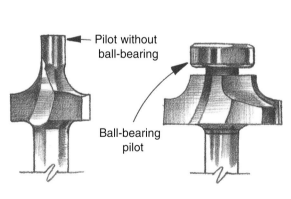

Pilot without ball-bearing

Ball-bearing pilot

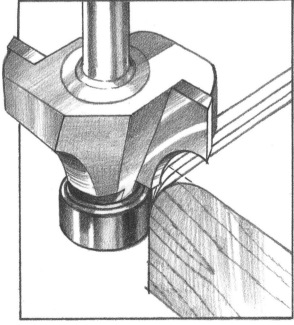

4 Don't get stalled on workpiece edges.

It sometimes can be difficult to start a router cut on the corner of a workpiece without easing the bit into the cut too slowly. To avoid burned corners, try to start the cut along an edge, then end the cut at the corner. If that's impossible, clamp a scrap block next to the starting corner, as shown *below.* (Note: the scrap must be the same thickness as the workpiece, and flush with its edge.) This way, you can start the cut in the scrap and rout through the corner without slowing.

5 Use a router table whenever possible.

A table-mounted router helps lessen your chances of accidental burning by giving you greater control over the workpiece as well as feed rate. Because you don't have to worry about running out of cord or balancing the router on the edge of a workpiece, you can concentrate on feeding the stock at a steady rate. For more detailed explanations of router tables and all their advantages, see Chapters 3 and 4.

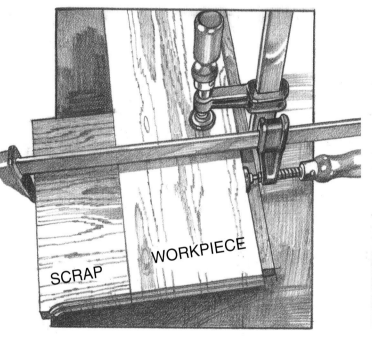

SCRAP

WORKPIECE

ROUTING STOPPED CUTS ON A ROUTER TABLE

Using a router table, you can cut one or more parallel slots or rabbets into a work-piece with optimal speed and precision. And, once you learn either or both of the two following procedures, you can stop those cuts precisely in any project you choose. For more information on router-table techniques, see Chapters 3 and 4.

First, a few basics

We already know that a "stopped cut" is any cut in a workpiece that starts at an outer edge and comes in but stops before reaching the other edge. This may sound simple, but getting them right takes the right procedure and a bit of practice.

There are a number of router bits available that will work well in making stopped cuts. A few of these include V-groove bits for one or more parallel veins, round-nose or "core-box" bits for cutting flutes, and dovetail bits for sliding-dovetail joints.

Most of the time, though, you'll use a straight or spiral bit to make square-walled cuts with flat bottoms. Depending on the application, you might be cutting a groove, rabbet, or mortise. For simplicity's sake, we'll refer to all of these cuts as "slots."

For both of the procedures described here, you'll need to do two things before getting started—first, adjust the height of the router-table bit to the proper cutting depth. (For deep mortises you may need to set the bit at a low starting height and make the cut in a series of passes.) Then, depending on where you want the cut to fall on the width of the workpiece, set the fence an appropriate distance from the bit.

Procedure 1: A fast, low-tech way to rout simple mortises

1 Mark the position of the cut onto the workpiece. Then, transfer the location of the end marks of the cut to the adjoining surface of your workpiece, as shown *below*. Next, transfer the marks to the surface opposite the surface to be cut.

3 Turn on the router and place the workpiece against the fence, with its left end suspended and its right end resting on the router table. Now, slowly lower the workpiece completely onto the router bit, with the workpiece's left mark about ½" to the left of the left mark on the fence, as shown *below*.

5 Now, slide the workpiece from right to left until the right marks on the workpiece and fence align. Then, slide the workpiece about ½" to the right and lift the workpiece straight up, taking care to keep it in firm contact with the fence. For slots more than 1" deep, turn off the router before removing the workpiece.

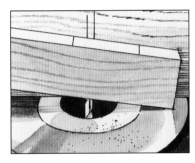

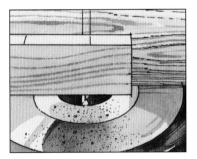

2 Use a square to mark the diameter of your router bit on the router-table fence. Rotate the router bit so that when you butt the square up to it, you mark the full cutting diameter.

4 Carefully slide the workpiece to the right so the left mark on the workpiece and left mark on the fence align. This short, so-called "climb-cut" goes opposite of typical feed direction, so go slow to ensure safety *and* accuracy.

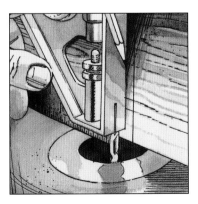

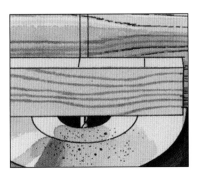

Procedure 2: Getting perfect results on multiple pieces

For fast, extremely accurate results with multiple workpieces, take a few minutes to position and clamp two stopblocks to the router-table fence. You can make the stopblocks from scrapwood. Just be sure to notch one corner—this will provide a place for sawdust to go so that your workpieces stay in good contact with the stopblock.

1 On a piece of scrap the same length as your workpiece, mark the position of the slot. Now, measure from the left end of the slot to the right end of the scrap. Use this measurement to locate a stopblock on the fence, measuring to the right from the left edge of the router bit. For example, the left end of the mortise shown here is 11⅝" from the right end of the scrap. So, we clamped the stopblock exactly 11⅝" from the left edge of the router bit.

2 On the same piece of scrapwood, measure from the right end of the mortise to the left end of the scrap (2⅝" in the example *below*). Use this measurement to position and clamp the left-side stopblock. As shown, we set the left-side stopblock exactly 2⅝" from the right edge of the router bit.

3 Start the router and place the scrap piece against the right-side stopblock, as shown *at bottom right*, and lower the piece onto the bit. Slide the piece to the left until it contacts the left-side block, then slide it back and forth to ensure a complete cut. Lift it straight up and measure the position of the slot. Adjust the stop-blocks as necessary before cutting your workpieces.

You may find that some workpieces are too long to rout using your current router-table fence. In that case, you can either make a longer fence or attach stop-blocks to the workpiece and cut the slots with a handheld router outfitteded with an edge guide.

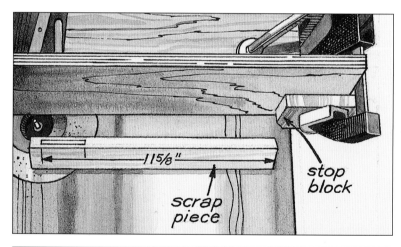

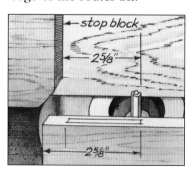

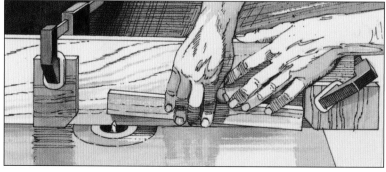

RAISED-PANEL DOORS

*Quality cabinets and casework furniture almost always sport raised-panel doors. And with a 1½-hp or larger router, a router table, and three bits (shown on **page 40**), they're quite easy to make.*

If you plan to make or remodel several cabinets or build special pieces of furniture featuring raised-panel doors, the cost of these expensive bits is well worth the investment. These horizontal bits cut with the workpiece lying flat on the router table, and produce impressive results compared to raised panels made on a tablesaw, or with the less-expensive vertical router bits for raised panels (see Chapter 6), which can't raise a panel with a desirable curved edge.

Two bits for the door frame ...

Coping bit + Sticking bit = Cope-and-stick joint

A set of door-making router bits makes it easy to build professional-quality cabinet doors. One bit cuts the coped shape at the ends of the rails; one cuts the sticking shape to match; and one cuts a raised field on the panel.

... and a third for the panel

Panel-raising bit

This large-diameter bit cuts the cove profile that "raises" the panel.

Choose a profile

The bits used in this project (available from woodworking tool and supply sources) form a set that includes a coping bit to cut the ends of the rails, a sticking bit to cut a matching profile and panel-holding groove on the inside edge of each rail and stile, and a 3½" diameter bit that "raises" the panel with a gently sweeping cove profile.

These bits all have ½" shanks, a better choice for this operation than ones having ¼" shanks.

See **Photos A**, **B**, and **C** for the shapes made by the rail-and-stile cutters, and how the results mate together.

Photo D shows one of the many panel-raising bit profiles available from several manufacturers. Choose the one you like best or that best matches the style of your home's existing cabinetry.

Select the very best stock

A great door can only come from great lumber. You want wood that shrinks and swells as little as possible, and resists warping. Rift-sawn or quarter-sawn lumber fills the bill here.

Inspect the stack of boards at your lumber supplier, looking at the end grain on each one. Select the ones with grain lines running straight from face to face, not from edge to edge or in a semi-circle. These prime boards also feature straight face grain, which is important for this door as you will see a little bit later.

You might find quite a bit of variation in one wide board, as shown in **Photo E.** In that case, give your work that extra touch of quality by selecting the straight grain lines for your doors. The wavy, flat (cathedral) grain won't go to waste—you can use it for less visible cabinet parts or other projects.

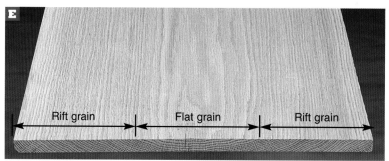

Rift grain | Flat grain | Rift grain

Here you see rift grain and flat grain within one 18" board. Plan to use the rift grain for visible parts and the flat grain elsewhere.

On a piece of cardboard, cut out a "window" the same size as the part you need to make. When you see the grain you want, mark the outline with chalk.

Once you've found a good board, don't just chop it into convenient lengths. Take one more big step toward master craftsmanship by cutting each individual piece with the straightest grain possible, as shown in **Photo F**.

Straight-grain rails and stiles seem to flow naturally around a door. We recommend straight grain for the panels, too. It lends an architectural-quality look.

We used red oak for this project because it's a popular cabinet choice and its prominent grain lines emphasize the difference in appearance between straight grain and random cathedral grain. Check out the two versions in **Photo G.** When you look at oak cabinets in a store, you'll notice a lot of figure, and maybe you prefer it that way. The choice is yours.

Two variations on red oak—the panel on the left was made with well-matched straight grain; the one on the right offers a more common appearance.

Plan and cut carefully

Here we built an overlay door for a standard-sized wall cabinet, which is common. We planed 4/4 stock to ¾" for our rails and stiles, and ripped them to 2¼" in width, a dimension that looks good, feels solid, and allows enough room for any style of hinge. You can choose a width anywhere from 1½" to 2½", but pick stock that's perfectly flat for the rails and stiles.

The door itself should fall between 9" and 18" in width—any narrower and it just won't look right. If you build it wider than 18", you're more likely to have trouble with twisting. The door must be absolutely flat to look good when it's closed.

An overlay door is typically used on cabinets without face frames. Size each door to nearly cover the cabinet box, and plan for a ⅛" gap between adjoining doors.

The sample door in **Drawing 1** will help you keep track of the slots and coped rail ends as you figure

the dimensions of your door. Check your crosscutting setup for accuracy before you cut the pieces, because the rails must be perfectly square for good results. You can prevent chip-out with an auxiliary fence on your miter gauge or a sacrificial piece of straight stock on the back fence of your crosscut sled. Cut an extra rail and an extra stile to use when setting bit heights.

To make the panel, choose boards with compatible color and figure, and plane them to a thickness of ½". Once you fit the panel into place, its surface will sit flush with the front of the frame.

Joint the edges of the boards, and then glue and clamp them together to make a slightly oversized blank.

1 TYPICAL DIMENSIONS

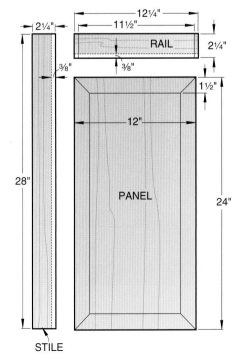

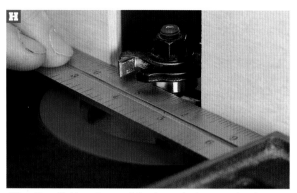

Align the pilot bearing and the fence before you begin rout-ing. This step will ensure a smooth cut with no dips in the workpiece.

For the rail-end cuts, set the height of the coping bit by eye. Place the top of its slotting cutter just proud of the workpiece.

After the glue dries, cut the panel to allow for a ⅛" gap all around as it sits in the grooves of the rails and stiles. This gap will accommodate the spacers described in "No-rattle panels" on *page 45, bot-tom*. If you choose not to use spacers, you must still leave the same gap to allow for wood movement.

Rout the rail ends

With your router mounted in a table, install the coping bit (it's the bit with a pilot bearing sandwiched between the two cutters). Hold a straightedge against the router-table fence, and slide the fence until the straightedge contacts the pilot bearing, as shown in **Photo H.** Now make sure the fence sits at a right angle to the miter gauge; butt a piece of scrap against the fence at one end, clamp it to your miter gauge, then slide the miter gauge along the fence. The scrap should maintain contact all along the length of the fence.

Use your test rail to set the height of the bit, as shown in **Photo I.** Place your test rail face side down on the table, one edge flat against the miter gauge auxiliary fence and one end touching the router-table fence. Hold the workpiece firmly against the auxiliary fence and down on the table, and rout the profile.

Check the test cut for a smooth, consistent shoulder about ¹⁄₁₆" thick on the face side of the rail. The rabbet on the opposite side will be about

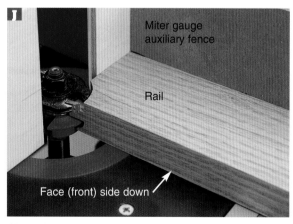

Keep the rail square to the router-table fence with your miter gauge and auxiliary fence. The auxiliary fence also helps prevent chip-out.

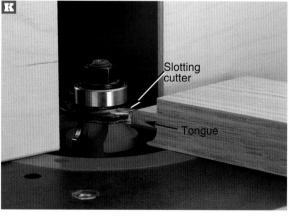

Use the coped end of a rail to set up the sticking cuts. Match the slotting cutter to the tongue, and if the curved profiles don't mate, re-shim the bit.

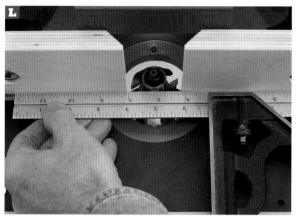

Again, line up the pilot bearing of the sticking bit and the router-table fence to ensure accuracy.

Make the long-grain cuts on all four frame pieces. Your fingers will be close to the bit, so be sure to keep your right hand at the outside corner as you push.

¼" deep. Run another test, if necessary, and when you're satisfied, make a set-up piece to keep for future projects. Now, rout both ends of each rail, as shown in **Photo J.**

Now, rout the inside edges

Remove the coping bit and install the sticking bit (the one with the pilot bearing on top) into your router. In one pass, this bit makes the frame look better by rounding over the edge next to the panel while simultaneously cutting the groove to receive the panel. Use one of the rails that you just routed to set the height. Match the slot-cutter with the tongue on the rail end, as shown in **Photo K.** Again, align the fence and pilot bearing with a straight-edge, as shown in **Photo L.**

Place your extra stile face side down against the router table fence, and make a test cut, as shown in **Photo M.**

Check its fit with the already routed rail. Place both pieces flat on your workbench or tablesaw top, face sides up, and check the resulting joint with your fingertips. Aim for a perfectly smooth joint because anything less will require a lot of sanding after assembly. So, do as many test runs as it takes to get it right, and then cut a set-up piece for future reference. See the Shop Tip on *page 44* for another way to save your settings.

If you can't get a perfect fit with the rails and stiles, you may have to adjust the bits themselves with very thin washer-like metal shims. Shims allow you to fine-tune the height of the profile cutters or the location of the tongue on the rail-end bit. Our bits came pre-shimmed from the factory, with extra shims held under the nut at the end of each bit. Write down each step if you do any shimming, so you know the

original arrangement as well as each adjustment that you make. When your test joints are right, rout the inside edge of all four frame pieces.

Time to raise the panel

For the final step in the milling process, use a panel-raising bit that measures 3½" in diameter. The large diameter means that it cuts more wood per revolution than the average bit, its outer edge travels faster than most, and it demands extra clearance in the table and fence.

For safety and efficiency, try to use a variable-speed router with at least 1½ hp. That's enough power to do the job, and running it at a low speed makes the operation safer.

Even if you have a split fence that opens wide enough to accommodate the bit, it's safer to shape a smaller opening in an auxiliary fence. A

SHOP**TIP**

Stop collar

Make your bits self-aligning

Wouldn't it be nice to keep your rail-and-stile profile cutters permanently aligned with one another, avoiding all those necessary test cuts every time you use them? Try this.

Slip a ½" stop collar onto the shank of each bit, and tighten it into place against the cutter body, as shown in the photo at left. Install the first bit into your router, and proceed to find the right height. Unplug the router, loosen the set screw on the collar, let it slide down to the collet, and retighten the set screw. Without changing the router height, do the same with the second cutter. The next time you use the cutters, use a

saved set-up profile to set the router height for the first cutter, and the second cutter will match automatically.

You can find stop collars at your local home center or hardware store, or in a mail-order catalog. For safety's sake, place at least 80 percent of a router bit's shank inside the collet. In this instance, you might consider collars that are ⁵⁄₁₆" thick.

---

wide gap causes problems if the workpiece slips into it.

To add an auxiliary wood fence, cut a piece of straight wood to size and mark the shape of the bit on it. Cut the opening on the bandsaw and smooth it with sandpaper. Attach the auxiliary fence to the existing fence, and check the bit clearance.

Align the bearing and fence, and make a test cut, as shown in **Photo N.** If the router bogs down, adjust the fence so the bit cuts less than the full width of the profile on the first pass. Then realign the bearing and fence, and shape the complete profile in another pass.

Test the fit of the panel tongue in the groove of a rail or stile. It should slide in easily. If you have to force it into the groove, raise the bit. If it rattles inside the groove, lower the bit.

When you find the right fit, rout the profile on the panel. Rout both ends first, then do the long sides; the long-grain cuts will shave off any minor chip-out from the end-grain cuts.

Tip: *Press downward on the workpiece as you rout, making sure that the shoulder around the panel field maintains a consistent depth.*

Stain the panel

Now that the door parts are milled, you are ready to prepare for assembly. You have allowed for wood movement in the solid panel during the planning phase. Carry through by installing spacers, as described in "No-rattle panels" on *page 45*, and by staining the panel, as in **Photo O,** if

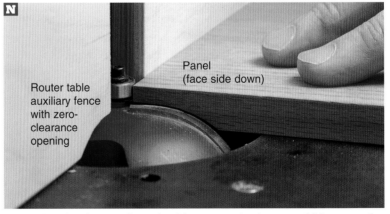

Router table auxiliary fence with zero-clearance opening

Panel (face side down)

Remember that the test pieces for this cut must be the same thickness as the panel. The tongue should fit snugly into the rail and stile grooves.

If you plan to stain your cabinet door, do the panel before assembly. The clear topcoat can wait until after assembly.

When you cut the rail ends square, and accurately match the coped and sticked profiles, assembly becomes almost automatic.

Don't stain the rails and stiles just yet. If stain gets onto the gluing surfaces, it may prevent the glue from adhering properly.

After the stain on the panel dries, insert the spacers and apply yellow glue to all of the surfaces that you milled on the rail end. Use only a light coating near the inside edge to keep squeeze-out away from the panel; even a weak bond there could cause problems.

Assemble the door and place it on two bar or pipe clamps, located to apply pressure across the width of the door at each end, as shown in **Photo P.** Measure diagonally between both pairs of opposing corners, also shown in the photo, to make sure the door is square. The two measurements should be equal. If not, loosen the clamps, slightly angle them to pull the frame into alignment, and retighten. Let the glue dry before staining the frame.

stain is part of your finishing plan. Stain the back first, and then place it on a support while you stain the face.

By staining the panel before assembly, you will ensure that the stain

completely coats the tongue of the panel. If you waited until after assembly, areas of the tongue might remain unstained, and could become visible when the panel shrinks in dry weather.

SHOP TIP

No-rattle panels

Solid-wood panels must have room to move because they absorb moisture in humid weather and lose it in dry times. If you simply leave a gap, you will wind up with a door that rattles and sounds poorly-made. Many kinds of foam are available to fill that gap, but a good product to try is "Space Balls." These firm rubber spheres, about ¼" in diameter, do the job quickly and neatly, and

they are available at most woodworking supply stores. Use two Space Balls on each side and each end of a small door, or three per side on a bigger one. Push the Space Balls into the grooves as far as you can. The panel will seat them during assembly. They'll compress when the panel expands, and return to full size as the panel shrinks, holding it tightly in its grooves year-round.

SPECIAL FEATURE: GIVE YOUR ROUTER A BREAK WHILE RAISING PANELS

Here's how to minimize the amount of wood removed by a panel-raising bit.

Take a piece of scrapwood and trace the profile of your panel-raising bit on it, as shown in Step 1. Then, using a sliding bevel gauge, find an angle that cuts away most of the waste without touching the desired profile. See Step 2 *below*. Lastly, set up your tablesaw with the sliding bevel, and run each side and end of the panel through as shown. This will make things a little easier on your router because there now will be much less wood to rout.

Note that you should set the rip fence away from the tilt of the blade. If you like, you can add a taller fence to the rip fence—this will help support the workpiece while you machine it on edge.

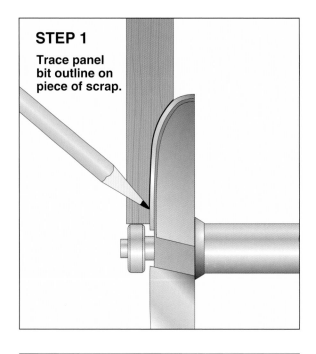

STEP 1

Trace panel bit outline on piece of scrap.

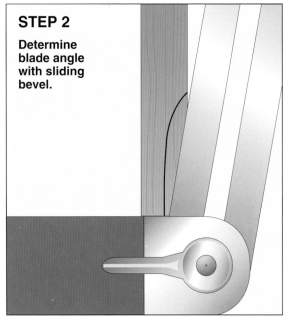

STEP 2

Determine blade angle with sliding bevel.

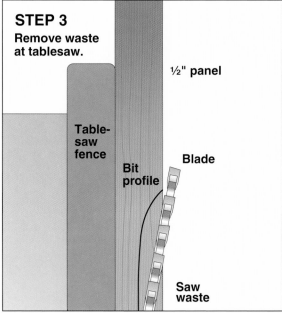

STEP 3

Remove waste at tablesaw.

½" panel

Table-saw fence

Bit profile

Blade

Saw waste

THE BASICS OF PLUNGE-ROUTING

Although first introduced in Germany more than 50 years ago, plunge routers weren't widely available in North America until the early 1980s. Now there are more models on the market than their fixed-base cousins.

Why take the plunge?

The plunge router's forte is making easier cuts on the interior surface (or *field*) of a workpiece for such tasks as mortising, stopped dadoes, inlay, and sign-routing. To make field cuts with a fixed-base machine, you need to tilt the spinning bit into and out of the cut—a tricky (and sometimes dicey) maneuver.

With a plunge router, the motor-and-bit mechanism slides up and down on two spring-loaded posts that are attached to the base. First you preset the cutting depth, and then release a lock that raises the motor and bit to a non-cutting height. Position the router over the cut, switch on the motor, and push it straight down until it contacts a depth-stop. Lock the plunge, make the cut, release the lock, and the motor and bit spring up again. You can even readjust the depth without turning off the router, which is useful for making multiple passes on deep cuts.

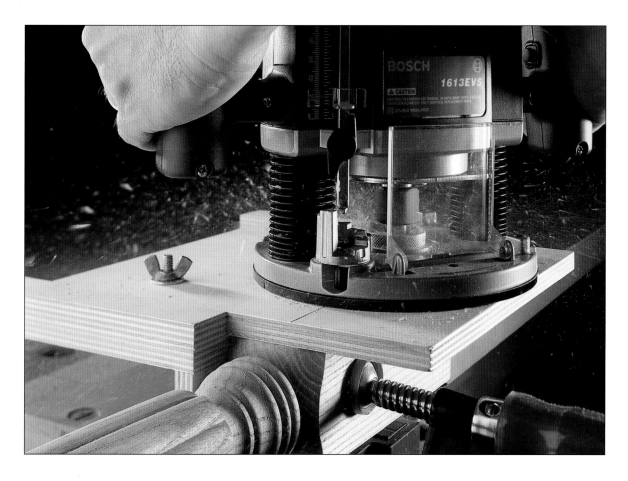

Plunge routers have their ups and downs

Sure, plunge routers might make quick work of some tricky cuts, but don't toss out your fixed-based router just yet. Here's why:

▣ PROS:

■ A plunge router is safer than a fixed-base model because its bit protrudes only when cutting.

■ Plunge routers typically offer more power—up to 15 amps—and most have variable-speed control, which fixed-base machines generally do not. These are major considerations if you plan to table-mount your router and work with large bits, such as panel-raisers.

■ For a table-mounted router, the plunge router's depth-adjustment knobs control bit-height changes more precisely. To take advantage of this feature, you may need to extend your router's height-adjustment knob. Several manufacturers include knob extensions with their plunge routers, or you can buy an extension for $20 or so.

▣ CONS:

■ Plunge routers cost and weigh more than fixed-base routers, and offer no advantage on edge cuts. If you anticipate making mostly edge cuts in your work, you may be better off purchasing a lighter and less expensive fixed-base tool.

■ Not all plunge routers work well suspended upside down beneath a router table. Falling dust can gum up unshielded plunge-posts, which you'll need to clean periodically.

■ When mounted in a table, adjusting the bit depth of some models can be an awkward, two-handed operation. With others, removing the plunge mechanism springs, which makes it easier to raise a table-mounted router, requires dismantling the machine's motor housing—a procedure we don't recommend.

Anatomy of a plunge router

Although they perform many of the same duties, plunge routers look distinctly different than fixed-base routers. In addition to the motor, collet, and handles—parts common to both styles—a plunge router also has the following:

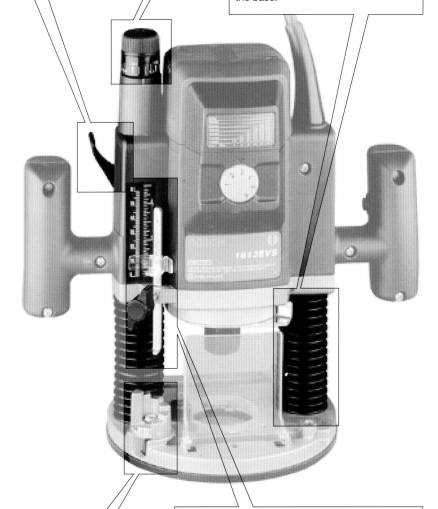

Plunge Lock
Tripping a lever, or squeezing or twisting a handle, locks the bit's depth after it has penetrated the workpiece. Releasing the lock lifts the bit at the end of the cut.

Micro-adjust
This feature fine-tunes the cutting depth with micrometer accuracy.

Plunge Rods
A pair of spring-loaded steel rods attached to the subbase guide the motor up and down, perfectly perpendicular to the base.

Turret Stops
For a project that requires progressively deeper cuts, such as routing deep mortises, you can preset the steps on a turret. Rotating the turret enables you to quickly step from one depth to the next.

Depth Adjustment Rod and Scale
Not all plunge routers offer a depth-of-cut scale, but all have an adjustable rod that helps you halt the plunge at a precise preset depth.
   With most plunge routers, you "zero" the tool by locking it at the point where the tip of a straight or spiral bit just touches the work surface. Then you set an adjustable cursor to "0" on the scale. The scale tells you the depth of the dado, mortise, or other cut you'll be making.

Six ways to plunge right in

To put a plunge router through its paces, you'll need the correct bit for the job at hand (manufacturers offer hundreds for different shapes and sizes of cuts) and some type of guide (straightedge, template, or jig). In many cases you'll also need guide bushings, which fit into your router's baseplate, to follow the guide.

You can spend a great deal of money on ready-made accessory jigs for your plunge router, or you can make your own for next to nothing. Here are six popular jigs for some useful plunge-routing tasks.

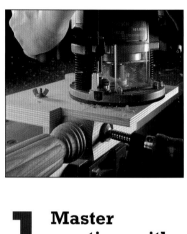

1 Master mortises with the help of this adjustable jig

The trick to cutting mortises in table legs is to precisely position the mortise on each leg and to make each mortise exactly the same length. Build the super-handy Mortising Jig, as shown in the drawing on the *left,* and you'll be able to cut identical ½"-wide mortises time after time.

To set up a cut, mark the mortise length and centerline on your workpiece. Clamp the workpiece to the jig's base so the mortise is centered in the slot on the sliding top plate. Lock the plate into place with the wing nuts. The threaded rod acts as a stop, and allows you to adjust the length of the mortise from ½" to 2¼". Once you've locked in these settings, you can transfer the jig quickly from one workpiece to the next.

Now, fit your router with a ¾" guide bushing and a ½" straight or spiral-flute bit.

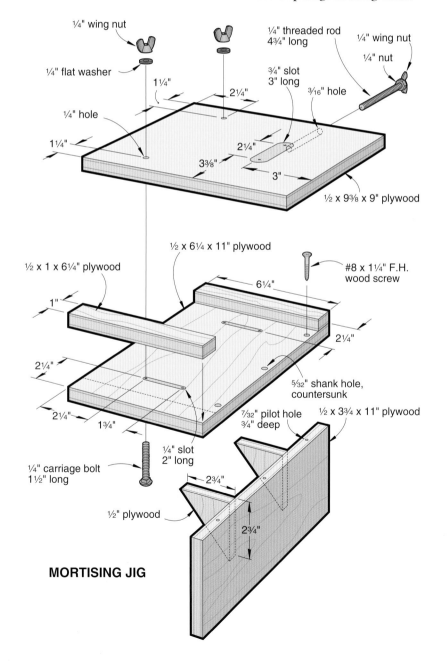

MORTISING JIG

(For the cleanest cuts, use an up-cut spiral for solid wood; a down-cut spiral for plywood and veneers.) Insert the guide bushing in the jig's slot, turn on the power, plunge, lock, and guide the router from one end of the slot to the other. Deep mortises will require two or more passes—no sweat, thanks to your plunge router's turret stops.

2 Stop, drop, and rout!

A plunge router excels at stopped cuts, such as slots, dadoes, and flutes. For stopped cuts in wide work-pieces, such as shelf dadoes in a bookcase, measure from the edge of your router's base-plate to the cutting edge of the bit. Clamp a straightedge guide that distance from where you want to dado, and a stop at each end of the cut. (Be sure to account for the bit-to-edge measurement on each end of the cut, but don't assume that measurement to be the same all the way around the base plate—your router's collet may not be perfectly centered within the tool's plate.)

For narrow workpieces such as the one shown in the photo at *top right,* use an edge guide that attaches to your router's baseplate. Clamp stopblocks at the ends of the cut as before.

3 A great jig for shelves and frames

While they are a sturdy way to hang such items as picture and mirror frames, shelves, and plaques, keyhole slots can spell trouble if they aren't exactly the same distance from the top of the project. You can go nuts offsetting the wall hangers to compensate for the misalignment.

KEYHOLE-ROUTING JIG

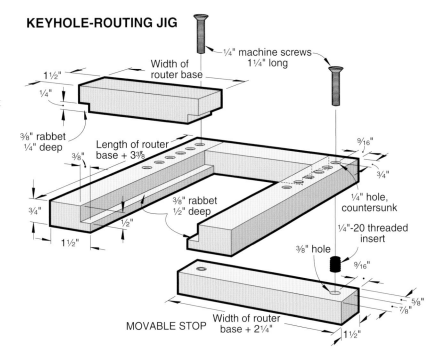

¼" machine screws 1¼" long

Width of router base

1½"

¼"

⅜" rabbet ¼" deep

Length of router base + 3⅜"

⅜"

¾"

⅜" rabbet ½" deep

½"

1½"

9/16"

¾"

¼" hole, countersunk

¼"-20 threaded insert

⅜" hole

9/16"

5/8"

7/8"

MOVABLE STOP   Width of router base + 2¼"

1½"

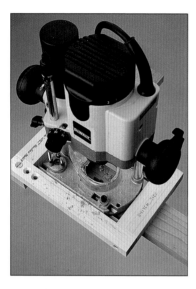

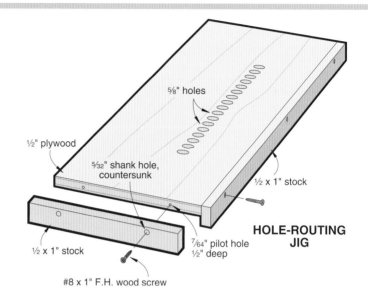

⅝" holes

½" plywood

⁵⁄₃₂" shank hole, countersunk

½ x 1" stock

HOLE-ROUTING JIG

½ x 1" stock

⁷⁄₆₄" pilot hole ½" deep

#8 x 1" F.H. wood screw

The keyhole-routing jig on *page 51* consists of a frame that fits your router's base. The router rides on the rabbets on each rail.

With the help of a movable stop, you can bore slots 6½", 7¼", or 8" from the top of the frame. After setting the stop, center and clamp the jig to one of the vertical frame pieces, place the router at the near end of the jig, plunge with a keyhole bit, slide it to the far end, then back out of the cut. Repeat the machining process on the other vertical frame piece.

4 Routing with templates: function follows form

With template routing, a shop-made pattern guides your router along cuts for making signs, shallow bowls, or trays. You also can use templates for carving lettering in wooden signs. One big advantage to template routing is that once you make the template, you can use it again and again to create absolutely identical cuts.

First, make a template—usually of ¼" hardboard or ½" plywood—of the pattern you wish to rout. Because you'll use a guide bushing to steer the router through the cut, you'll need to cut the template pattern slightly larger than the finished pattern. How much larger, you ask?

Just subtract the diameter of your router bit from that of the guide bushing, and divide the difference by two. Add that measurement to all sides, then cut out the template with your bandsaw or scrollsaw, removing the template pieces you want to remove from the workpiece.

Clamp or affix the template with double-faced tape to the workpiece, rout clockwise around the perimeter of the template, and clean out the center with back and forth passes.

Here's another neat way to use a template and guide bushing with your plunge router: When you need to bore a series of identically spaced holes, such as for shelf pins, make a template like the one shown on *page 52,* and you'll do the job more efficiently and chip-free, even in melamine. Size the template holes to accommodate the guide bushing. (We used a ⅝" bushing with a ¼" down-spiral bit.) **Note:** *Remember to bore the holes* before *assembling the cabinet. Refer to page 173 of the appendix for sample template holes.*

is limited to making raised panels with medium-density fiberboard (MDF) which you plan to paint rather than applying a clear-finish.

The Panel-Routing Guides, shown *below,* amount to a simple frame with splined corners that let you adjust it to a variety of panel sizes. Cleats on the back of the frame capture the panel. And to keep the router from tipping toward the field and ruining the cut,

tape a small disc the same thickness as the guides to one corner of the router's base with double-sided tape.

Here, we made the cuts with a plunge-ogee bit, but you also can use a bearingless ovolo or plunge bead bit. You also can create bevels and coves up to 1½" wide with bigger 3½" raised-panel cutters, but these are best used in a router table.

5 Raise panels with a plunge

A router removes stock, so how can it *raise* a panel? Actually, plunging with a bearingless bit into the field of a flat panel creates the illusion of frame-and-panel construction. Note that this technique

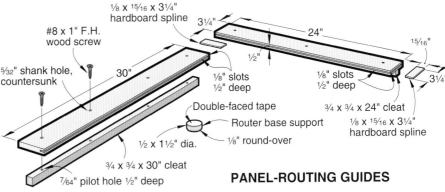

⅛ x ¹⁵⁄₁₆ x 3¼" hardboard spline

#8 x 1" F.H. wood screw

3¼"

24"

½"

¹⁵⁄₁₆"

⁵⁄₃₂" shank hole, countersunk

30"

⅛" slots ½" deep

⅛" slots ½" deep

3¼"

Double-faced tape

Router base support

⅛" round-over

½ x 1½" dia.

¾ x ¾ x 24" cleat

⅛ x ¹⁵⁄₁₆ x 3¼" hardboard spline

¾ x ¾ x 30" cleat

⁷⁄₆₄" pilot hole ½" deep

PANEL-ROUTING GUIDES

6 Swing a wide arc, or make compact discs

Here are two ways to help your plunge router get around. With the Disc-Routing Jig, shown *below right,* you can use different combinations of bits and bushings to cut discs in diameters from 2⅛"–6" in ⅛" increments.

Make the template as shown, using a fly-cutter in your drill press. Because the size of the template holes must be exact, make sure to test each cut in scrap first. To avoid chip-out in the finished cuts, cut the holes to about half of their depth, flip the template over, place the center bit into its hole, and complete the cut. You'll find the mini-charts (showing which bit and bushing to use) for each template hole in the appendix on *page 173.* Using these will allow for dead-on precision.

For routing larger circles and arcs, build and outfit your router with the Circle-Cutting Trammel, shown *below left,* that cuts circles up to about 72" in diameter. Note that the jig's two steel rods slide into the router's subbase.

Set the radius of your arc or circle by measuring from the cutting edge of the bit to the center pin on the jig, and lock in the radius along the threaded knobs. Insert the pin into a predrilled hole at the center of the workpiece, and use the trammel like a giant compass. With thicker or harder stock, you may need to make this cut in several progressively deeper passes.

Leery about drilling a center hole that might mar your project? Try drilling and cutting from the back or underside of the workpiece.

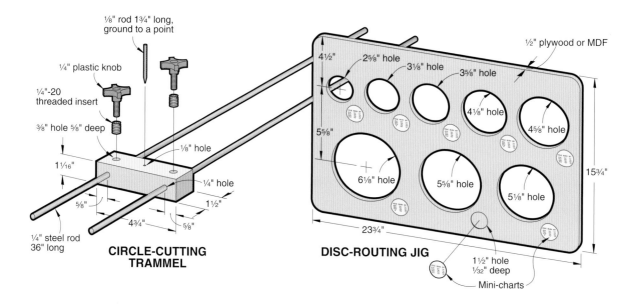

⅛" rod 1¾" long, ground to a point

¼" plastic knob

¼"-20 threaded insert

⅜" hole ⅝" deep

1 1/16"

⅛" hole

¼" hole

⅝"

1½"

4¾"

⅝"

¼" steel rod 36" long

CIRCLE-CUTTING TRAMMEL

½" plywood or MDF

4½"

2⅝" hole

3⅛" hole

3⅝" hole

4⅛" hole

4⅝" hole

5⅝"

6⅛" hole

5⅝" hole

5⅛" hole

15¾"

23¾"

DISC-ROUTING JIG

1½" hole 1/32" deep

Mini-charts

FOUR GREAT ROUTER TRICKS

Although there's no sleight of hand involved in working with a router, there are ways to charm more uses from it. Try these shop-proven techniques and presto! You'll achieve some magical results.

1 Rout louvers in no time

Traditional louvered-door (or shutter) construction techniques can be fairly complicated and time-consuming. This jig, a plunge router, and a tablesaw make building a louver insert for a frame a pretty easy procedure.

It's a good idea to build the insert first and then make the frame. That way, you can make minor adjustments in the size of the frame's opening to fit the insert—a much simpler process than building a louvered insert to exact size. Follow these steps to make the insert's stiles and rails:

STEP 1: Plan the number of louvers (each louver takes up 1" of the stile's length).

Beautiful and functional louvers like these are just a router jig away.

Materials List

| Part | Finished Size | | | Mat. | Qty. |
	T	W	L		
A	¾"	6½"	23"	P	1
B	¾"	1⅛"	3"	H	1
C	¾"	3"	5"	H	1
D	¾"	4"	4"	P	1
E	½"	*	**	H	2
F	½"	1"	**	H	2
G	½"	1"	2¼"	H	2

Material Key: P—plywood, H—any hardwood

*Width of router base +2"

**Length of router base +4 ¾"

LAYING OUT SLOT SPACING

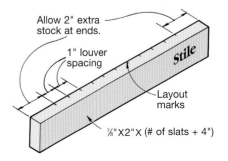

Allow 2" extra stock at ends.

1" louver spacing

Stile

Layout marks

⅞"X2"X (# of slats + 4")

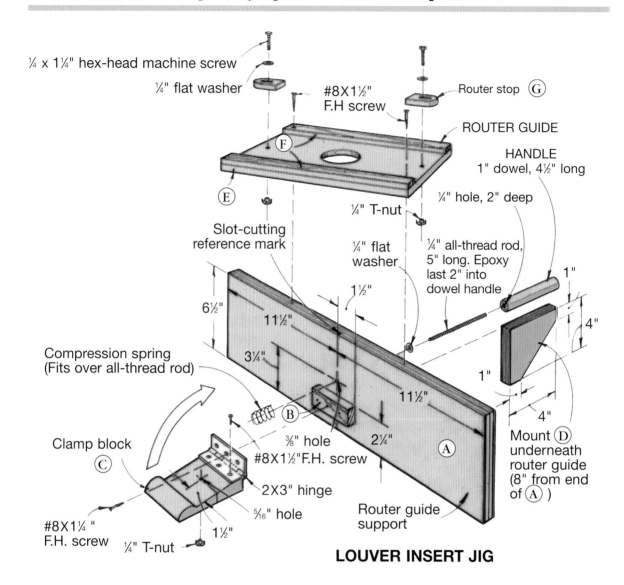

¼ x 1¼" hex-head machine screw

¼" flat washer

#8X1½"
F.H screw

Router stop (G)

ROUTER GUIDE

HANDLE
1" dowel, 4½" long

¼" hole, 2" deep

F

E

Slot-cutting
reference mark

¼" T-nut

¼" flat
washer

¼" all-thread rod,
5" long. Epoxy
last 2" into
dowel handle

1½"

6½"

11½"

3¼"

1"

4"

Compression spring
(Fits over all-thread rod)

11½"

1"

Clamp block
C

⅜" hole
#8X1½"F.H. screw

2¼"

A

4"

Mount (D)
underneath
router guide
(8" from end
of (A))

B

2X3" hinge

#8X1¼ "
F.H. screw

⁵⁄₁₆" hole

Router guide
support

¼" T-nut

1½"

LOUVER INSERT JIG

You can size the louver jig to accept
any plunge router.

STEP 2: Machine a piece of
stock that's ⅞" thick, 2" wide,
and to length. (See the Laying
Out Slot Spacing drawing.)
Then, lay out the spacing of
the slots that hold the louvers.

STEP 3: Clamp a piece of
⅞" scrap stock into the jig by
placing the wood between
the clamp block and router
guide support. Secure the stock
by tightening the handle.

Now, set the jig stops (G) for
the 1¹⁄₁₆"-long slot, as shown
at *on the opposite page.*

STEP 4: With a straight bit,
make an ¹¹⁄₁₆"-deep test cut,
lowering the bit in ⅛" passes.

STEP 5: When satisfied
with your test cuts, clamp the
stile stock into the jig, aligning the first louver mark with
the jig's reference mark. Cut a
slot at each louver mark.

SETTING LENGTH OF SLOT

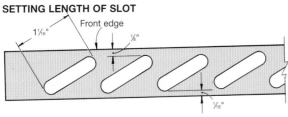

1¹⁄₁₆"   Front edge   ⅛"   ¹⁄₁₆"

STEP 6: With the slot-side of the stock facing the fence, rip the stock into two ¼"-thick stiles, as shown on *page 58 in the upper left photo.*

STEP 7: From the leftover stock, rip the ¼"-thick rails.

STEP 8: With a ⅛" round-over bit, shape the inside and outside front edges of the rails and stiles. Leave the back edges square.

STEP 9: Miter the rails and stiles (start the stile miters ¹⁄₁₆" from the top and bottom slots).

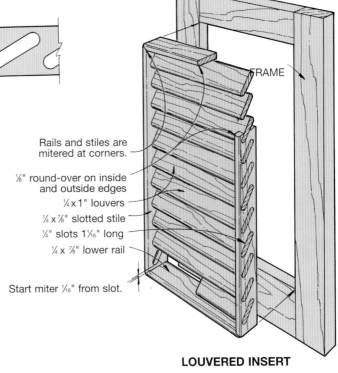

FRAME

Rails and stiles are mitered at corners.

⅛" round-over on inside and outside edges

¼ x 1" louvers

¼ x ⅞" slotted stile

¼" slots 1¹⁄₁₆" long

¼ x ⅞" lower rail

Start miter ¹⁄₁₆" from slot.

LOUVERED INSERT

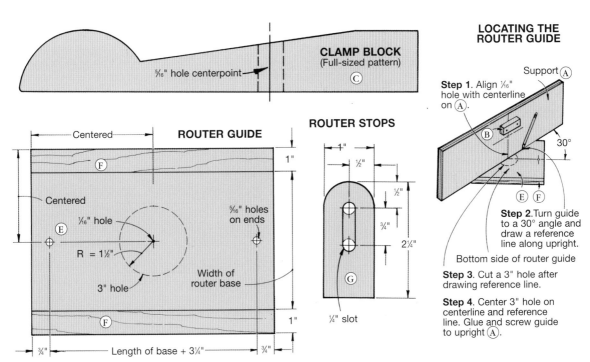

CLAMP BLOCK
(Full-sized pattern)

⁵⁄₁₆" hole centerpoint

C

ROUTER GUIDE

Centered

1"

Centered

¹⁄₁₆" hole

E

R = 1½"

3" hole

⁵⁄₁₆" holes on ends

Width of router base

F

F

1"

¾"   Length of base + 3¼"   ¾"

ROUTER STOPS

1"

½"

½"

¾"

2¼"

G

¼" slot

LOCATING THE ROUTER GUIDE

Support A

Step 1. Align ¹⁄₁₆" hole with centerline on A.

B

30°

E   F

Bottom side of router guide

Step 2. Turn guide to a 30° angle and draw a reference line along upright.

Step 3. Cut a 3" hole after drawing reference line.

Step 4. Center 3" hole on centerline and reference line. Glue and screw guide to upright A.

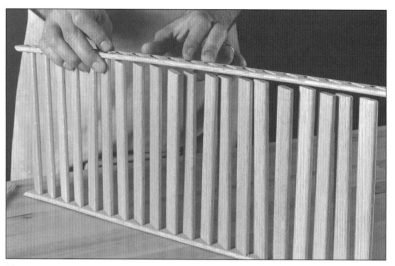

Rip both stiles from one workpiece, then rip the rails.

Use a gentle hand to attach the stiles to the louvers. To avoid splitting the stiles, remachine any louvers that don't fit.

To make the louvers, first rip a ¼"-thick test strip from a piece of 1"-thick stock. Round off all four edges of the strip with a ⅛" round-over bit, and check its fit into the louver slots. Adjust your tablesaw and router until the test strip fits in the slots. Now, cut the louver stock to lengths ¹⁄₁₆" shorter than the rails and assemble the louvers and stiles, as shown at *top right.* Be patient as you insert the louvers into the stiles—the stiles may split if you try to force a louver that's too large into them. Glue the rails into place.

2 Create simple frames with a rabbeting bit

Cabinet door frames don't have to be a hassle. Try this technique with ¾"-thick stock for rails and stiles with ⅜" rabbeted edges that make strong joints. The rabbet accommodates a plywood panel or ⅛" glass with ¼" stops, as shown *below.*

A router provides you an easy way to make attractive frames with smooth, clean rabbets.

First, set a ⅜" rabbeting bit for a ⅜"-deep cut. To test this, cut a few scrap blocks from the frame stock and adjust the bit's depth until it removes exactly one-half of the thickness of the stock. Refer to the photo of the scraps shown *at middle left* that shows some test results.

Now, refer to the drawing at *top right* as a guide, and cut the stiles to length and the rails to the width of the frame opening plus ¾" to allow for the two ⅜" rabbets. Rout a rabbet along one of the long edges on the backside of each piece. Then, flip the rails over and clamp them to your workbench. Before rabbeting each end of both rails, you must align the ends of the rails flush with the scrap blocks so the bit's pilot has a straight surface to ride on. This arrangement prevents the router from tearing out the corners of the workpieces or rounding them off, as shown *middle right*.

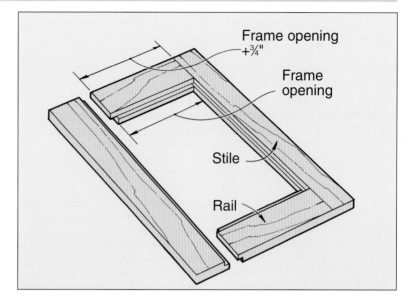

Frame opening +¾"

Frame opening

Stile

Rail

Our tests produced, from left, a too-shallow cut, a correct cut with flush faces, and a too-deep cut.

Scrap blocks

Scrap blocks (one with a rabbet) provide a straight, continuous surface for the bit's pilot to ride on.

3 Save time with a flush-trimming jig

There are several ways to flush-trim edge banding applied to a plywood panel, but this jig proves highly versatile and easy to use. Plus, it not only trims flush along straight edges, but it's also good at working its way into corners.

Once you build the jig and

A flush-trimming jig saves you hours of planning and scraping.

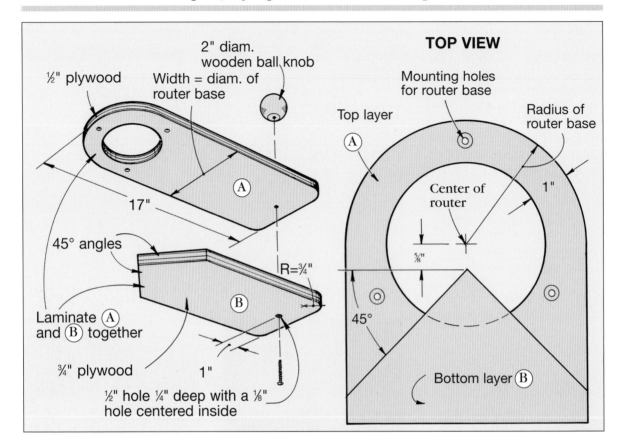

TOP VIEW

½" plywood

2" diam.
wooden ball knob

Width = diam. of
router base

17"

45° angles

R=¾"

Laminate Ⓐ
and Ⓑ together

¾" plywood   1"

½" hole ¼" deep with a ⅛"
hole centered inside

Ⓐ

Ⓑ

Mounting holes
for router base

Top layer

Ⓐ

Radius of
router base

Center of
router

⅝"

1"

45°

Bottom layer Ⓑ

attach your router to it, insert a ½" hinge-mortising bit and adjust it so it's just a hair above the plywood surface. Keep a steady hand on both the wooden knob and router handle to give a flat surface.

4 Draw circles using templates

Draftsmen's templates enable you to draw circles much faster than with a compass. Here's an adaptation that allows you rout circles nearly as quickly. You can use this system to cut 28 different-sized circles from a template with only seven holes!

To make a template for

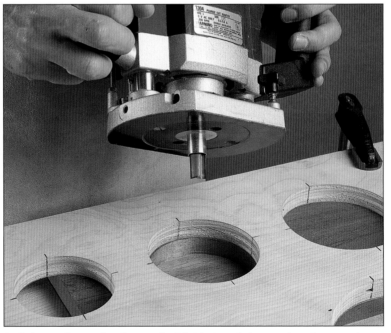

A circle template makes fast work of flat-bottom holes, such as the one above, as well as through-holes.

routing holes from 2⅝" to 6" in diameter, in ⅛" increments, first lay out the circles' centers where shown in the drawing, *below right,* on a 15 × 23" piece of ¾" plywood. Because the size of the seven template holes must be exact, test each cut in scrap stock with a circle cutter before cutting the template holes. The photo at *bottom* shows cutting the holes in the template. To avoid chip-out on the back side of the

template, cut the holes to about half of their depth, flip over the template, place the center bit into its hole, and complete the cut.

With all the holes cut, extend the four centerline marks down the walls of each hole with a try square. These marks help you center the template holes over the layout lines on your workpiece. Now, mark the diameter of each template hole and save a copy

of the chart *below left.* This helpful chart shows what size straight router bit and guide bushing to use for each desired hole size.

In addition to cutting holes through stock, a router also will cut flat-bottom holes. When doing this, you may find that your router base doesn't span some of the larger template holes. When that occurs, make a 12"-diameter auxiliary base of ¼" clear acrylic.

Make 28 sizes of holes with one template			
Desired hole size	Template hole	Guide bushing	Bit size
2⅝	Hole 1 3⅛" diam.	¾	¼
2¾		⅝	¼
2⅞		⅝	⅜
3		⅝	½
3⅛	Hole 2 3⅝" diam.	¾	¼
3¼		⅝	¼
3⅜		⅝	⅜
3½		⅝	½
3⅝	Hole 3 4⅛" diam.	¾	¼
3¾		⅝	¼
3⅞		⅝	⅜
4		⅝	½
4⅛	Hole 4 4⅝" diam.	¾	¼
4¼		⅝	⅜
4⅜		⅝	¼
4½		⅝	½
4⅝	Hole 5 5⅛" diam.	¾	¼
4¾		⅝	¼
4⅞		⅝	⅜
5		⅝	½
5⅛	Hole 6 5⅝" diam.	¾	¼
5¼		⅝	¼
5⅜		⅝	⅜
5½		½	½
5⅝	Hole 7 6⅛" diam.	¾	¼
5¾		⅝	¼
5⅞		⅝	⅜
6		⅝	½

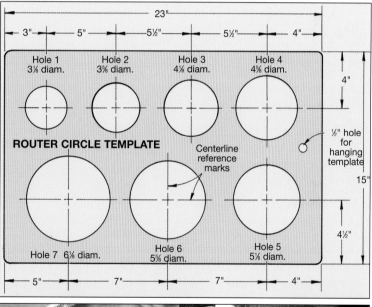

23"
3" — 5" — 5½" — 5½" — 4"

Hole 1 3⅛ diam. Hole 2 3⅝ diam. Hole 3 4⅛ diam. Hole 4 4⅝ diam.

ROUTER CIRCLE TEMPLATE

Centerline reference marks

Hole 7 6⅛ diam. Hole 6 5⅝ diam. Hole 5 5⅛ diam.

5" — 7" — 7" — 4"

4"

½" hole for hanging template

15"

4½"

Cut the template holes with a 6" circle cutter. After cutting each hole to half its depth, flip over the stock and complete the cut to avoid chip-out.

3 Router Table Options

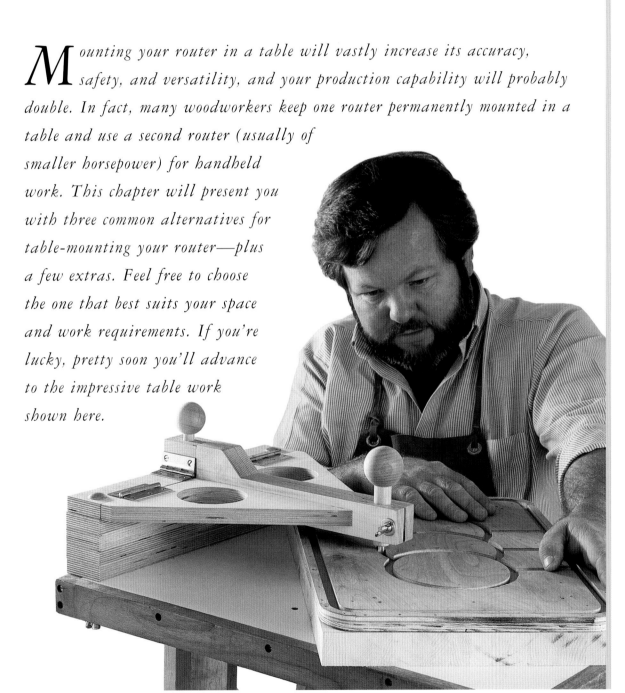

*M*ounting your router in a table will vastly increase its accuracy, safety, and versatility, and your production capability will probably double. In fact, many woodworkers keep one router permanently mounted in a table and use a second router (usually of smaller horsepower) for handheld work. This chapter will present you with three common alternatives for table-mounting your router—plus a few extras. Feel free to choose the one that best suits your space and work requirements. If you're lucky, pretty soon you'll advance to the impressive table work shown here.

ADDING A ROUTER EXTENSION TO YOUR TABLESAW

Adding a router-table extension to your contractor-style tablesaw is fairly easy to accomplish—simply remove the metal extension that's there now, and then build and bolt this one into place.

Important note: *This table was built for a specific 10" saw model, so the dimensions and connections may vary somewhat for your saw.*

As a general rule, you should plan to make the tabletop as wide as the extension being replaced and as long as the front and rear rails can sturdily support. Sometimes, the extension table can be slightly longer than the metal extension it replaces.

Constructing the tabletop assembly

Note: The letters referenced herein refer to the illustrations on page 65.

1 Cut the extension tabletop (A) to size from ¾" plywood.

2 Cut the banding strips (B, C) to size, mitering the ends as shown in the drawing on the *opposite page*.

3 To mount the banding strips to the plywood, drill and countersink mounting holes through the strips and into the tabletop edges. Making sure the top edges are flush, glue and

screw the strips to the table-top. Sand the top surface of the banding flush with the top of the plywood tabletop.

4 Measure the length and width of the banded top, and cut a piece of plastic laminate to the measured size *plus 1"* in length and width. Using contact cement, center and adhere the plastic-laminate to the top of the tabletop assembly (A, B, C).

5 Fit your router with a flush-trimming bit, and rout the edges of the laminate flush with the edges of the banding.

6 Follow Steps 1 through 5 on the Tabletop Layout drawing *(page 66)* to form the opening in the tabletop for the router plate. (Tip: when routing the ⅜" rabbet ⅜" deep in Step 5, it's a good idea to go ⁵⁄₁₆" deep on the first pass, and then ¹⁄₆₄" deeper per pass until the top surface of the plate is perfectly flush with

the top surface of the table-top laminate. (Your other option is to have a piece of ⅜" acrylic cut to size.)

Materials List

| | Finished Size | | | Matl. | Qty. |
Part	T	W	L		
A tabletop	¾"	15½"	25½"	BP	1
B banding	¾"	1½"	27"	M	2
C banding	¾"	1½"	17"	M	2

Material Key: BP-birch plywood, M-maple.
Supplies: #8 x 1¼" flathead wood screws, 18 x 28" plastic laminate, contact cement, ⅜ x 7¾ x 10¼" clear acrylic insert, bolts and flat washers for mounting extension table to saw table.

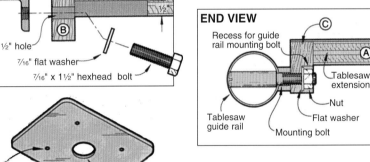

FRONT VIEW
Tablesaw table
(A)
Tablesaw extension
½"
½" hole
(B)
⁷⁄₁₆" flat washer
⁷⁄₁₆" x 1½" hexhead bolt

END VIEW
(C)
Recess for guide rail mounting bolt
(A)
Tablesaw extension
Nut
Tablesaw guide rail
Flat washer
Mounting bolt

EXPLODED VIEW (from below the table

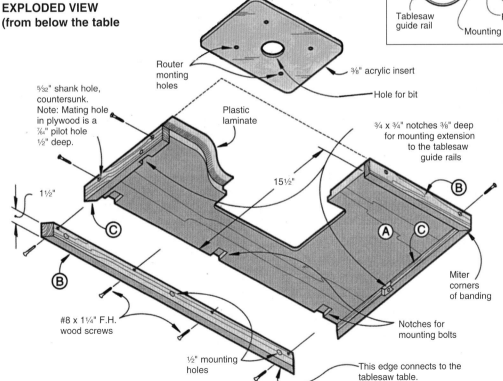

Router monting holes
⅜" acrylic insert
Hole for bit

⁵⁄₃₂" shank hole, countersunk. Note: Mating hole in plywood is a ⁷⁄₆₄" pilot hole ½" deep.

Plastic laminate

¾ x ¾" notches ⅜" deep for mounting extension to the tablesaw guide rails

1½"

15½"

(C)

(A) (C)

(B)

Miter corners of banding

#8 x 1¼" F.H. wood screws

½" mounting holes

Notches for mounting bolts

This edge connects to the tablesaw table.

Mounting the extension to the saw table

1 Follow the four-step drawing *below* to mark the mounting holes in the tablesaw extension. Before drilling, double-check that the top surface of the extension table will be perfectly flush with the top surface of your saw table.

2 Use a chisel to form notches (1½"-wide by 1¾"-long by ½"-deep) on the bottom side of the extension for housing the hexhead bolts. See the Front View drawing on *page 65* for reference. Fasten the extension to the saw table.

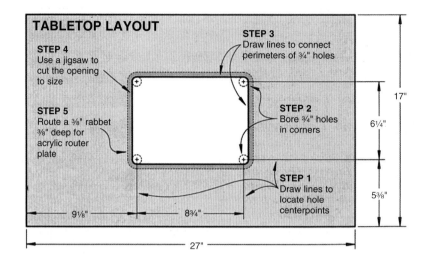

TABLETOP LAYOUT

STEP 4 Use a jigsaw to cut the opening to size

STEP 5 Route a ⅜" rabbet ⅜" deep for acrylic router plate

STEP 3 Draw lines to connect perimeters of ¾" holes

STEP 2 Bore ¾" holes in corners

STEP 1 Draw lines to locate hole centerpoints

17"

6¼"

5⅜"

9⅛"

8¾"

27"

3 Using the holes in the guide rails as guides, mark their location onto the outside surfaces of both banding pieces (C). Remove the extension table from the saw table and drill the guide-rail mounting holes where marked. See the End View for reference. Chisel a notch

(⅜"-deep) on the inside face of the banding strips (the mounting bolts aren't long enough to go completely through the ¾"-thick banding).

4 With the top edges perfectly flush, fasten the extension table to the saw table and rails.

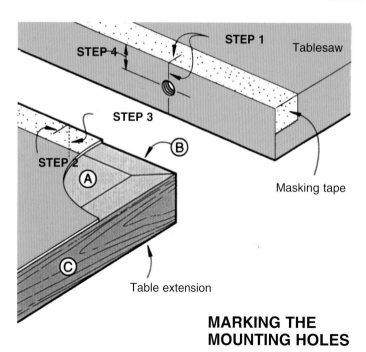

STEP 1

STEP 4

STEP 3

STEP 2

Ⓐ

Ⓑ

Ⓒ

Tablesaw

Masking tape

Table extension

MARKING THE MOUNTING HOLES

STEP 1
Mark and transfer the centerlines from the saw-table holes to masking tape.

STEP 2
Position the extension table against the saw table, and transfer the marks.

STEP 3
With a square, extend the lines down the edge of the table extension banding (B).

STEP 4
Measure the distance from the top of the saw table to the centerline of the existing hole. Transfer that dimension to the table extension. Drill the mounting holes through the banding.

THE BENCHTOP ROUTER TABLE

A benchtop router table gives you the best of two worlds—full service and portability. Look around and you'll find many commercial benchtop router tables advertised, but you can build this feature-packed one in a weekend for the same or less money.

Great features of this model:

- A fence that adjusts in a flash and locks in place with the twist of a knob.

- A mini-track in the fence for quick and solid positioning of your homemade feather boards and router bit guard.

- Levelers ensure a perfectly aligned tabletop.
- A dust-collection port to minimize debris.
- A total weight of 36 pounds —it even travels well!

1 TABLE EXPLODED VIEW

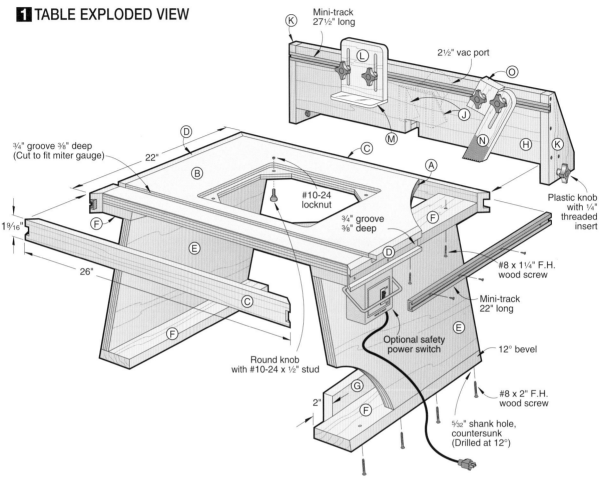

Mini-track 27½" long

2½" vac port

¾" groove ⅜" deep (Cut to fit miter gauge)

22"

#10-24 locknut

¾" groove ⅜" deep

Plastic knob with ¼" threaded insert

1⁹⁄₁₆"

26"

#8 x 1¼" F.H. wood screw

Mini-track 22" long

Optional safety power switch

12° bevel

#8 x 2" F.H. wood screw

Round knob with #10-24 x ½" stud

⁵⁄₃₂" shank hole, countersunk (Drilled at 12°)

2"

First, start at the top

1 Cut both a piece of birch plywood for the panel (A) and a piece of plastic laminate for the skin (B) an inch larger in length and width than the sizes listed in the Materials List (see *page 69*).

2 Following the directions on the can, apply contact adhesive to the back of the laminate and the face of the plywood. Bond the laminate to the plywood, holding the laminate about ⅛"

back from one edge and one end of the plywood, as shown in the shop tip on *page 71*. Apply pressure with a rubber laminate roller.

3 With the plywood's exposed end and edge against your tablesaw's rip fence, trim about ¼" off the panel's opposite end and edge, cutting through both the plywood and laminate. Now with the newly-trimmed end and edge in turn against the fence, cut the panel/skin (A/B) to finished size.

1a SECTION DETAIL

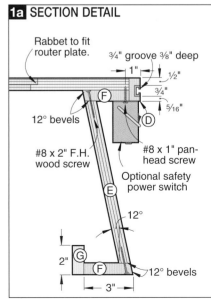

Rabbet to fit router plate.

¾" groove ⅜" deep

1"

½"

¾"

⁵⁄₁₆"

12° bevels

#8 x 2" F.H. wood screw

#8 x 1" pan-head screw

Optional safety power switch

12°

2"

12° bevels

3"

4 Cut the edge bands (C) and the end bands (D) to width, but about 1" longer than the lengths listed. Miter-cut them to fit around the top, as shown in **Drawing 1.** Glue and clamp them in place, keeping their top edges flush with the laminate's surface, as shown in the shop tip on *page 73*.

5 Install a ¾" dado blade in your tablesaw, and attach a tall (about 10") auxiliary fence to the rip fence. Adjust the blade and fence to cut the grooves in the end bands (D) for the mini-track, as shown in **Drawing 1a**. Test your setup with a piece of scrap and make any necessary adjustments. With the laminated side against the fence, cut the mini-track grooves in the end bands (D). Back up your cuts with a follower block to eliminate chipping as the blade exits the workpiece.

1b TABLETOP

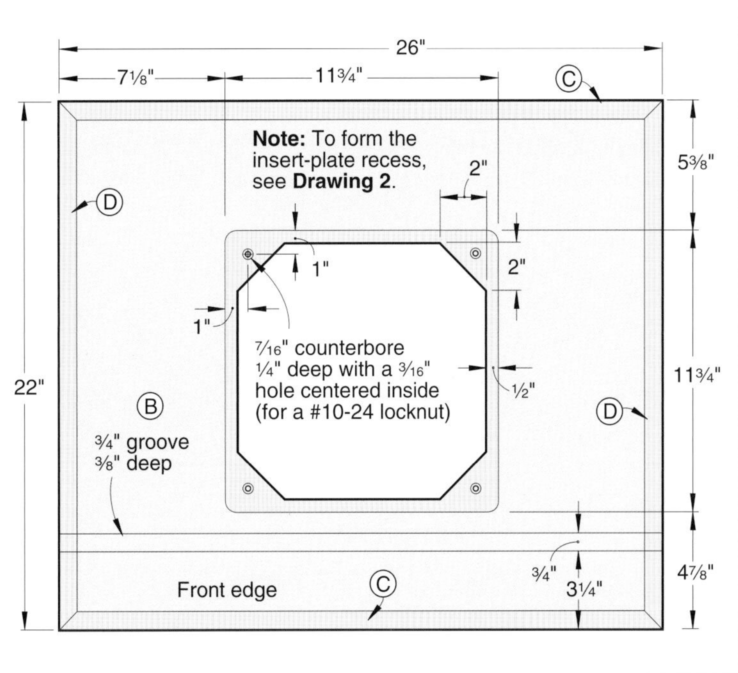
26"
7⅛"
11¾"
Ⓒ
Ⓓ
Note: To form the insert-plate recess, see Drawing 2.
2"
5⅜"
1"
2"
1"
7/16" counterbore ¼" deep with a 3/16" hole centered inside (for a #10-24 locknut)
½"
22"
Ⓑ
11¾"
Ⓓ
¾" groove ⅜" deep
Front edge
Ⓒ
¾"
3¼"
4⅞"

Materials List

	Finished Size T	W	L	Matl.	Qty.
Table					
A* panel	¾"	20½"	24½"	BP	1
B* skin	1/16"	20½"	24½"	PL	1
C* edge bands	¾"	1 9/16"	26"	M	2
D* end bands	¾"	1 9/16"	22"	M	2
E* legs	¾"	11½"	20½"	BP	2
F* leg cleats	¾"	3"	20½"	M	4
G cord cleat	¾"	2"	16½"	M	1
Fence					
H* fence	¾"	6"	26 1/32"	M	1
I* fence base	¾"	3"	26 1/32"	M	1
J vac port mounts	¾"	2½"	3⅛"	M	2
K fence brackets	¾"	4¾"	7½"	M	2
Guard & Feather board					
L guard base	¾"	5"	5"	M	1
M guard	¼"	2¾"	5"	A	1
N*feather boards	¾"	1¾"	8"	M	2
O jam blocks	¾"	1¾"	3"	M	2

*Parts initially cut oversize.

Materials Key: BP–birch plywood, PL–plastic laminate, M–maple, A–acrylic.

Supplies: #8×1¼" flathead wood screws, #8×1½" flathead wood screws, #8×2" flathead wood screws, #8×1" panhead screws, #8×1" brass flathead wood screws (2), ¼" SAE flat washers, contact adhesive, 5-minute epoxy, #10-24 locknuts (4). ¼" hex-head bolts 1½" long (8), knobs with ¼" threaded inserts (8), miniature knobs with #10-24×½" studs (4), 36" mini-track with screws (1), 24" mini-tracks with screws (2), 2½" vac port (1), ⅜×12×12" acrylic insert plate (1), safety power switch.

6 With the same dado blade, cut a groove in a piece of scrap, and test the fit of your miter-gauge bar. It should slide freely with very little play. Make any necessary adjustments. With the laminated side face down, cut the miter-gauge groove in the top, as shown in **Drawing 1b**. Back up the cut with a follower block to eliminate chipping.

Fit the insert plate and install plate levelers

1 Follow the eight steps in **Drawing 2** to create the square insert-plate recess in the tabletop.

STEP 1: Trim the insert plate to the size shown, and position it 4⅞" from the tabletop's front edge and centered side-to-side.

STEP 2: Trace an outline of the plate onto the tabletop.

STEP 3: Mark the opening cutlines inside the outline.

STEP 4: Drill a blade start hole, and use your jigsaw to cut the opening.

STEP 5: Secure the insert plate inside your traced outline with double-faced tape.

STEP 6: Clamp the guide boards around the insert plate, spacing each board away from the plate with business-card shims.

STEP 7: Remove the insert plate and shims. Chuck a

straight bit with a top-mounted pilot bearing (pattern bit) into your handheld router. With its base resting on top of the guide boards, adjust the router to cut ⅛" into the tabletop.

STEP 8: Guiding the bit's pilot bearing along the guide board's inside edges, begin routing the recess. Make additional passes, lowering the bit each time until you reach a depth of about 1/32" greater than the thickness of the insert plate.

2 FORMING THE INSERT-PLATE RECESS

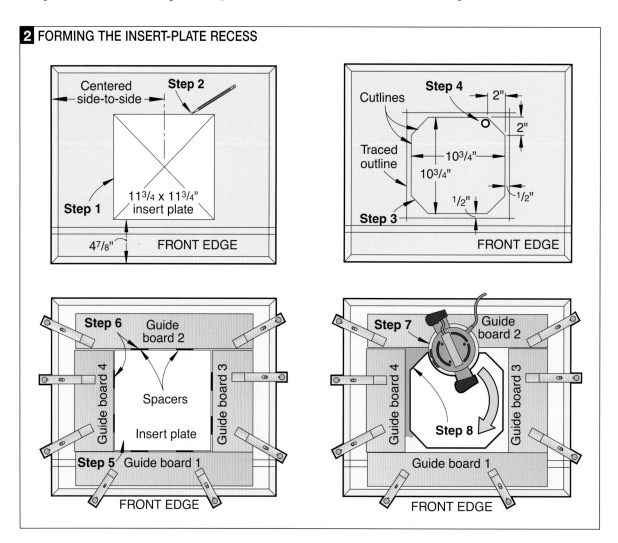

2 With the insert-plate recess formed, drill ⁷⁄₁₆" counterbores ¼" deep in each corner for #10-24 lock-nuts, as shown in **Drawing 1b** *(page 69)*. Make sure that, when placed in the counterbores, the locknuts are flush with the surface of the recess. Drill ³⁄₁₆" holes through the centers of the counterbores.

3 Referring to the sidebar "How to add insert-plate levelers to your table" on *page 75,* fasten epoxy locknuts into the counterbores. Finish-sand the bands (C, D) to 220 grit. Ease the sharp laminate edges of the miter-gauge slot and insert-plate recess with a cabinet scraper or sanding block.

Build a sturdy base

1 Cut the legs (E) and leg cleats (F) to length, but about 1" wider than listed. Tilt your tablesaw blade 12°, and

Cutting Diagram

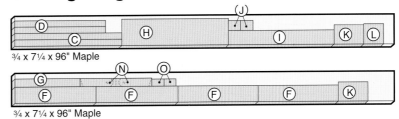

¾ x 7¼ x 96" Maple

¾ x 7¼ x 96" Maple

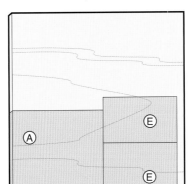

¾ x 48 x 48" Birch plywood

¼ x 2¾ x 5"
Acrylic

Ⓑ

21½ x 25½"
Plastic laminate

bevel-rip the edges of the legs and leg cleats, as shown in **Drawing 1a**. Cut the cord cleat (G) to size.

2 Glue and clamp the leg cleats (F) to the legs (E). Then, drill pilot and countersunk shank holes through the leg cleats into the legs. Drive the screws and remove the clamps. Glue and clamp the cord cleat to the leg cleat. Finish-sand the leg assemblies to 220 grit.

SHOP**TIP**

Flush trimming with your tablesaw

When applying plastic laminate to a tabletop panel, start with oversized pieces of plywood and laminate. Apply contact cement to both the laminate and the plywood. Position the laminate just shy of one edge and end of the plywood, as shown in the photo. Run these edges, free of overhanging laminate, against your tablesaw fence first when trimming the top to its finished size. Cutting both plywood and laminate at the same time avoids router flush trimming.

Note: *When storing the router table, coil the router and switch cords and stow them under the table, wedging them between the leg and the cord cleat.*

3 Place the top assembly upside down on your bench. Glue and clamp the leg assemblies to the top. Drill pilot and countersunk shank holes through the leg cleats into the top. Drive the screws.

Build an accurate fence

1 Forming straight, square edges on your parts is essential for making a straight fence. Start by cutting the fence (H) and the fence base (I) ½" wider and 1" longer than the sizes listed. Joint one edge of each board. Next, set the fence on your tablesaw ⅟32" over the finished width, and rip the parts. Set your jointer's depth to ⅟32" and joint the freshly cut edge. Check the length of your tabletop and *add ⅟32"* to this measurement. Cut the fence

and fence base to this length. (The added ⅟32" allows the fence to slide easily.) Bandsaw centered bit-clearance notches (1½X1½") in both parts. Glue and clamp the fence and base together.

2 Cut two blanks to ¾ x 4¾ X 7½" for the fence brackets (K). Fasten the two blanks together with double-faced tape. Mark the diagonal cut and the location of the ¼" hole on the top blank, as shown in **Drawing 3a**. Bandsaw and sand to the marked line, and drill the hole. Separate the brackets.

3 FENCE EXPLODED VIEW

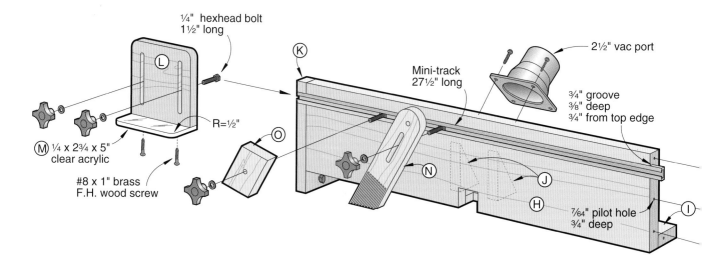

¼" hexhead bolt 1½" long

Ⓛ

Ⓜ ¼ x 2¾ x 5" clear acrylic

R=½"

#8 x 1" brass F.H. wood screw

Ⓞ

Ⓚ

Mini-track 27½" long

Ⓝ

Ⓙ

Ⓗ

2½" vac port

¾" groove ⅜" deep ¾" from top edge

7/64" pilot hole ¾" deep

Ⓘ

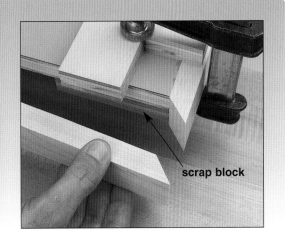

SHOP**TIP**

Keep your banding flush and corners aligned

Make alignment blocks by cutting 2 x 2" notches out of four 4 x 4" pieces of ¾" plywood. (The notches will allow you to see the mitered corners.) Clamp them to the top, as shown in the photo at *right*. Use scrap blocks beneath the top so as to space the clamps away from the banding. Now, glue and clamp the banding to the top, keeping it tight against the alignment blocks.

scrap block

3 Glue and clamp the fence brackets (K) to the fence (H/I), making sure the brackets' edges are flush with the fence's face. Drill pilot and countersunk shank holes through the brackets into the fence, as shown, and drive the screws. With your dado blade adjust-ed to the width of the mini-track, cut the dado in the fence (K/H/K), as shown in **Drawing 3**. Next, finish-sand the fence assembly through 220 grit.

4 Cut the vac port mounts (J) to the size and shape shown in **Drawing 3b**.

Dry-position the mounts and check their placement with your vac port. Glue and clamp the mounts into place. With the glue dry, use the port to mark the mounting screw locations. Drill the screw pilot holes and set the vac port aside for now.

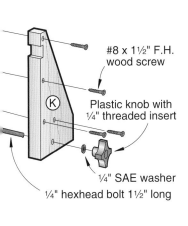

#8 x 1½" F.H. wood screw

Plastic knob with ¼" threaded insert

Ⓚ

¼" SAE washer

¼" hexhead bolt 1½" long

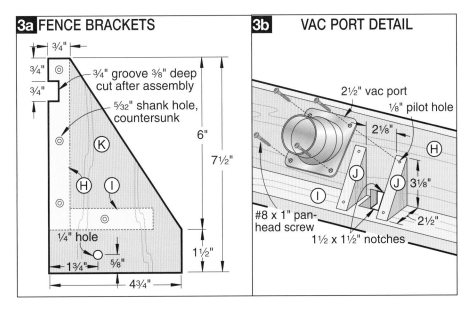

3a FENCE BRACKETS

¾"
¾"
¾"
¾" groove ⅜" deep cut after assembly
⁵⁄₃₂" shank hole, countersunk
Ⓚ
Ⓗ Ⓘ
6"
7½"
¼" hole
1¾" ⅝"
1½"
4¾"

3b VAC PORT DETAIL

2½" vac port
⅛" pilot hole
2⅛"
Ⓗ
Ⓙ Ⓙ
Ⓘ
3⅛"
2½"
#8 x 1" pan-head screw
1½ x 1½" notches

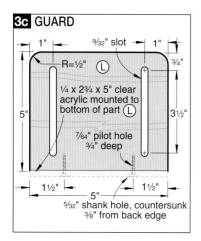

3c GUARD

1"   9/32" slot   1"
R=½"   (L)   ¾"
¼ x 2¾ x 5" clear
acrylic mounted to
bottom of part (L)   3½"
5"
7/64" pilot hole
¾" deep
1½"   1½"
5"
5/32" shank hole, countersunk
⅜" from back edge

Now, get your guard up

1 Cut the guard base (L) to size. Sand the ½" radii on the top corners, as shown in **Drawing 3c**. To form the mounting slots, drill 9/32" holes, where shown; draw lines from hole to hole; and scrollsaw along the lines. Finish-sand the base through 220 grit.

2 Cut ¼" acrylic to size for the guard (M). Disc-sand ½" radii on the outside

corners, as shown in **Drawing 3**. Adhere the guard to the base with double-faced tape, keeping the back edges flush. Drill pilot and countersunk shank holes through the guard (M) into the base (L). Remove the guard and set it aside.

Make the handy feather boards

1 Select a straight-grained piece of ¾"-thick maple, and cut a ¾ X 2 X 18" blank for the feather boards. Using your tablesaw and miter gauge, trim 30° angles on both ends of the blank, as shown in **Drawing 4**. Mark angled lines across the blank's width (2⅝" from each end) and mark the feather boards' radius ends.

2 Install a regular (⅛" wide) blade in your tablesaw and raise it 2" high. Set the rip fence 1/16" from the blade. With the long edge of the blank against the fence, cut in to the marked line, then *carefully* pull the board straight back from the

blade. *Note: A padded jointer pushblock works well for this operation.* Flip the board end over end and repeat. Reset the fence at ¼" and repeat the cut on each end. Repeat cutting the feathers at 3/16" intervals up to 1¾". With the fence set at 1¾", lower the blade to 1", and cut the blank to its finished width.

3 Drill the 9/32" hanging and slot-starting holes in the feather boards (N), as shown in **Drawing 4**. Mark and scrollsaw the slots, and bandsaw the rounded ends. Finish-sand the feather boards to 220 grit.

4 Cut the jam blocks (O) to size and drill the centered 9/32" holes. Finish-sand them to 220 grit.

Note: Jam blocks are positioned against the feather boards to prevent them from pivoting when applying pressure to a workpiece.

4 FEATHER BOARDS & JAM BLOCK

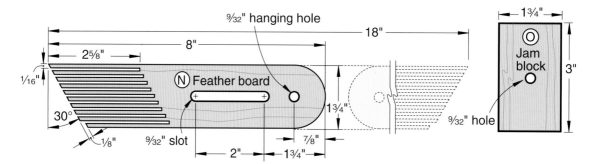

9/32" hanging hole
18"
8"
2⅝"
1/16"
(N) Feather board
1¾"
30°
1¾"
⅛"   9/32" slot
2"   1¾"   ⅞"

1¾"
(O)
Jam block   3"
9/32" hole

SHOP**TIP**

Make a self-gauging feather board

Here's a quick way to set your feather board to apply the proper pressure. Trim the first feather ⅛" shorter than the others, as shown in **Drawing 4.** When you use your feather board, place this short gauging feather on top of your workpiece. Now, keeping the other feathers parallel to the router-table top, tighten the mounting knob.

Lastly, apply a finish and install the hardware

1 Touch up the finish sanding where needed. Apply two coats of a penetrating oil finish to all wood parts, including the miter-gauge slot and the insert-plate recess (follow the instructions on the can). An oil finish is easier to reapply than paint or varnish. It also seals the miter-gauge slot and insert-plate recess without building up and interfering with the fit.

2 Hacksaw a mini-track to the lengths of the table ends and fence. You'll have to drill and countersink new mounting holes at the cut ends. Using the holes in the mini-track as guides, drill pilot holes into the table and fence, and screw the track into place.

3 Mount the optional switch, as shown in **Drawings 1** and **1a**.

4 Screw the guard (M) to the guard base (L) with #8x1" brass flathead wood screws. Attach the assembled guard, feather boards, and jam blocks to the fence, and then the fence to the table with hexhead bolts, washers, and knobs as shown. Now screw the vac port to the mounts.

5 Screw the insert-plate leveling knobs into the locknuts. Sand the insert plate's corners to match the corners of the insert recess.

How to add insert-plate levelers to your table

Adjusting your router table's insert plate perfectly flush with the top is as easy as installing locknuts in the corners of the plate's recess. Once you've drilled counterbored holes to accept #10-24 nuts in all four corners, here's how to proceed.

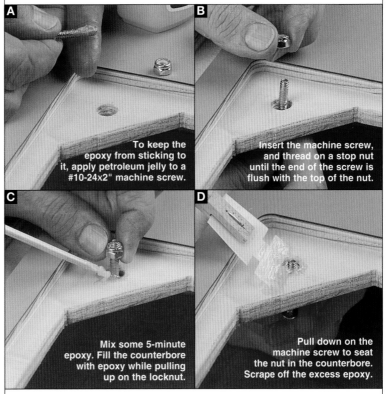

A To keep the epoxy from sticking to it, apply petroleum jelly to a #10-24x2" machine screw.

B Insert the machine screw, and thread on a stop nut until the end of the screw is flush with the top of the nut.

C Mix some 5-minute epoxy. Fill the counterbore with epoxy while pulling up on the locknut.

D Pull down on the machine screw to seat the nut in the counterbore. Scrape off the excess epoxy.

When the epoxy hardens, replace the 2"-long machine screw with a ½"-long one. For no-tool adjustment, use a knob with a ½"-long threaded stud.

THE ALL-PURPOSE ROUTER STATION

Used horizontally, this router table is great for mortise-and-tenon work. Crank it vertically (with ease) for other tasks. Plus, the same crank raises and lowers the plunge router! (This requires a flat and unobstructed housing top). <u>Important note:</u> *This is a fairly complicated project, and not one we would recommend for amateur woodworkers.*

Start with the cabinet and the tables

1 Because you're going to need four studded knobs later in the project, you might as well make them now. To make the knobs, cut four 2½" lengths of ⅜" threaded rod and epoxy them into four plastic knobs. Set the knobs aside while the epoxy cures.

2 Cut the base (A) and sides (B) to the sizes listed in the Materials List *(page 79).* Drill four ⅜" holes in the base, as shown on the Cabinet Base drawing on *page* 77. Cut rabbets in the bottom edges of the sides, drill the ⅜" holes, and form the ⅜ X ¾" slot, as shown in the Parts View—Side drawing on *page 176.* The slot is located only on the right side. Glue and screw the sides to the base, as shown in the Cabinet Assembly drawing on *page 78,* keeping the sides square to the base.

3 Cut the table front/back skirts (C), side skirts (D), auxiliary side skirts (E), and auxiliary back skirt (F) to size. Form the rabbets in the ends of the front/back skirts (C), rout the stopped slots in the side skirts (D), and drill the ⁷⁄₁₆" holes in the side skirts (D) and auxiliary side skirts (E), as shown in the Table Assembly and Auxiliary Table Assembly drawings *(below* and *page 79)*. To form the stopped slots in the side skirts (D), chuck a ⅜" straight bit in your table-mounted router and raise it to

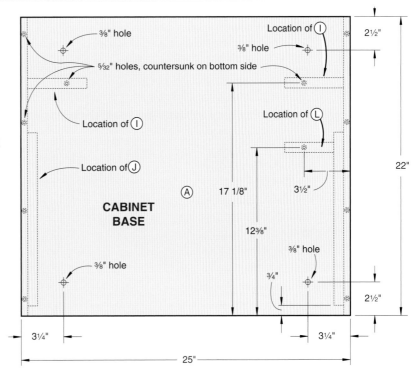

cut ⅛" deep. Position the fence to center the bit on the width of the skirts. Limit the cut by clamping stopblocks to the fence. With one end against the right stopblock, lower the skirt onto the running bit and rout the length of the slot. Repeat this process, raising the bit ⅛" with each pass until you rout the slot through. Install the T-nuts in the side skirts (D) and auxiliary side skirts (E).

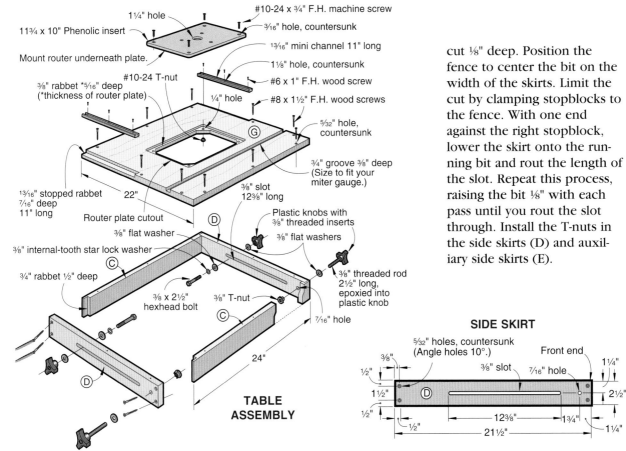

CABINET ASSEMBLY

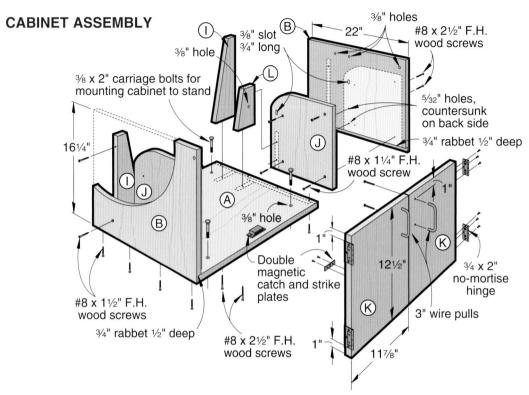

3⁄8" slot 3⁄4" long

3⁄8" hole

3⁄8 x 2" carriage bolts for mounting cabinet to stand

3⁄8" holes

22"

#8 x 2½" F.H. wood screws

5⁄32" holes, countersunk on back side

3⁄4" rabbet ½" deep

16¼"

#8 x 1¼" F.H. wood screw

1"

3⁄8" hole

Double magnetic catch and strike plates

12½"

1"

3⁄4 x 2" no-mortise hinge

#8 x 1½" F.H. wood screws

3⁄4" rabbet ½" deep

#8 x 2½" F.H. wood screws

1"

11⁷⁄8"

3" wire pulls

4 Drill pilot and counter-sunk shank holes, and screw the frames together, as shown in the Table Assembly and Auxiliary Table Assembly drawings. Cut the top (G) and auxiliary top (H) to size, and clamp them to the frames C/D and C/E/F, making certain the frames are square. Drill pilot and counter-sunk shank holes, as shown, and screw and glue the tops to the frames.

***Note:** The length of the table assemblies C/D/G and C/E/F/H must be the same dimension as the distance between the cabinet sides (B), minus the thickness of two business or playing cards for operating clearance.*

5 Rout grooves in the top (G) and auxiliary top (H) to match the bar on your miter gauge, as shown in the Parts View and Auxiliary Table Assembly drawings. Set the auxiliary table aside. Rout stopped rabbets in the rear edges of the top (G), and square the ends with a chisel.

Next, form a recess for the insert

1 Trim the insert to size, and center it on the top (G), as shown in the Parts View—Top drawing on *page 177.* Draw a line around it in pencil. Remove the insert. Cut four 3⁄4 x 6 x 16" particle-board routing guides, and clamp two of them in place aligned with two adjacent sides

of the marked outline. Replace the insert, and position and clamp the other two guides in place, as shown in **Photo A** *(page 80)*. Remove the insert.

2 Position spacer strips (3⁄8" thick, 3⁄4" wide) around the inside of the opening formed by the rout-ing guides. Secure 3⁄4"-thick, 45° triangles, 2" long on the diagonal, in the corners with double-faced tape. Chuck a ½" top-bearing pattern bit in your handheld router. Starting with the depth of cut set at 1⁄8", and increasing the depth of cut 1⁄8" with each pass, make repeat-ed passes to cut out an open-ing in the center of the top, as shown in **Photo B** *(page 80)*. Remove the spacer strips and triangles.

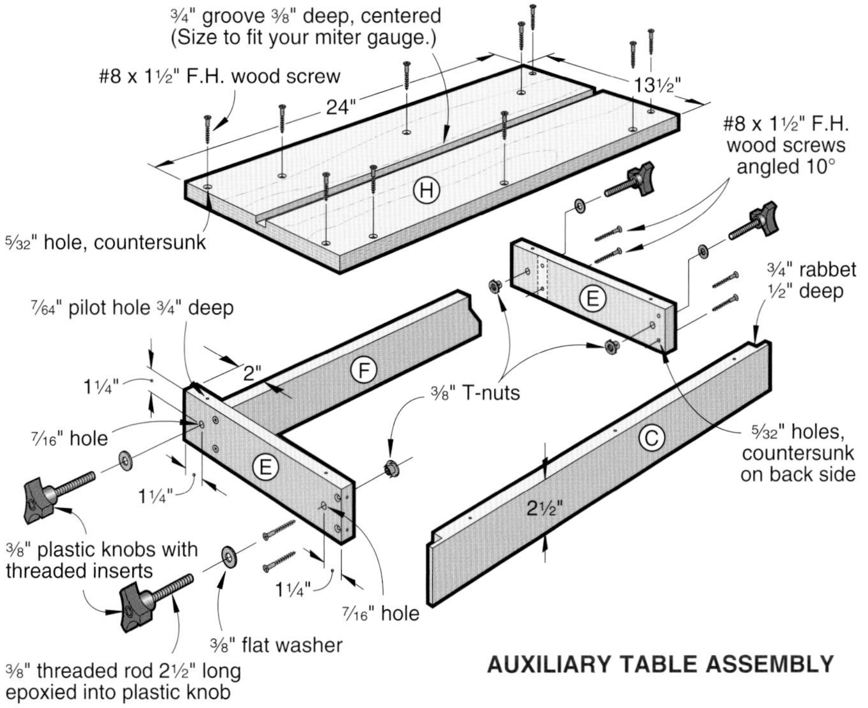
3/4" groove 3/8" deep, centered
(Size to fit your miter gauge.)
#8 x 1 1/2" F.H. wood screw
24"
13 1/2"
#8 x 1 1/2" F.H.
wood screws
angled 10°
H
5/32" hole, countersunk
3/4" rabbet
1/2" deep
7/64" pilot hole 3/4" deep
E
F
2"
1 1/4"
3/8" T-nuts
7/16" hole
C
5/32" holes,
countersunk
on back side
E
1 1/4"
2 1/2"
3/8" plastic knobs with
threaded inserts
1 1/4"
7/16" hole
3/8" flat washer
3/8" threaded rod 2 1/2" long
epoxied into plastic knob

AUXILIARY TABLE ASSEMBLY

Materials List

Part	Finished Size T	W	L	Matl.	Qty.
A base	3/4"	22"	25"	BB	1
B sides	3/4"	22"	16 1/4"	BB	2
C front/back skirts	3/4"	2 1/2"	24"	M	3
D side skirts	3/4"	2 1/2"	21 1/2"	M	2
E auxiliary side skirts	3/4"	2 1/2"	13 1/4"	M	2
F auxiliary back skirt	3/4"	2 1/2"	22 1/2"	M	1
G top	3/4"	22"	24"	BB	1
H auxiliary top	3/4"	13 1/2"	24"	BB	1
I* braces	3/4"	4 1/2"	12 3/4"	BB	2
J* table guides	3/4"	12 3/4"	12 3/4"	BB	2
K doors	3/4"	11 7/8"	12 1/2"	BB	2
L arm block	3/4"	3 3/4"	6"	BB	1
M** lift arms	3/4"	7 7/8"	12 5/8"	BB	2
N wrist pin	1" diameter		2 1/8"	D	1
O** crank	3/4"	2 1/8"	6"	BB	1
P discs	3/4"	2 1/8" diameter		BB	4
Q fence face	3/4"	3"	24"	BB	1
R fence base	3/4"	2 5/8"	24"	BB	1
S fence blocks	3/4"	2 1/8"	2 1/8"	BB	2
T vac port	1/4"	3 3/4"	4"	H	1
U stop bases	3/4"	1"	1 1/2"	M	2
V stopblocks	5/8"	1 1/2"	4"	M	2

* These pieces are cut from the same blank.
** Part initially cut oversize.

Materials Key: BB–Baltic birch plywood, M–maple, D–hardwood dowel, H–tempered hardboard.

Supplies: #6x1" flathead wood screws (15), #8x1 1/4" flathead wood screws (14), #8x1 1/2" flathead wood screws (50), #8x2 1/2" flathead wood screws (5), 3/8x2 1/2" hexhead bolts (2), 3/8x3" hexhead bolt, 3/8x4 1/2" hexhead bolt, 3/8x2" carriage bolts (4), #10-24x3/4" flathead machine screws (4), 3/8" T-nuts (6), #10-24 T-nuts (4), 3/8" lock nuts (5), 3/8" hex nuts (4), 3/8" coupling nut, 3/8" flat washers (26), 3/8" nylon washer, 3/8" internal-tooth star washers (2), 13/32x13/16" mini channel (2 @ 11", 1@ 24" long) plastic knobs with 3/8" threaded inserts (11), 3/8" threaded rod (4 @ 2 1/2", 1 @ 9" long), 3/8x1 1/2" square-head bolts (5), 3/8x11 3/4x11 3/4" phenolic sheet, 3/4x2" no-mortise hinges (4), 3" wire pulls (2), double magnetic catch and strike plates, 1 1/4" wood knob, epoxy, clear finish, primer, paint.

CUTTING DIAGRAM

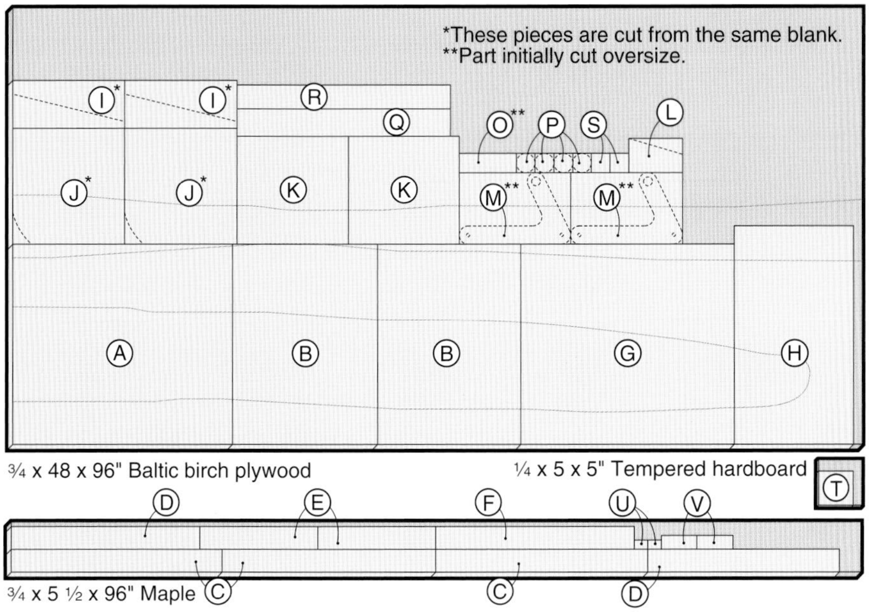
*These pieces are cut from the same blank.
**Part initially cut oversize.
I*
I*
R
Q
O**
P
S
L
J*
J*
K
K
M**
M**
A
B
B
G
H
3/4 x 48 x 96" Baltic birch plywood
1/4 x 5 x 5" Tempered hardboard
T
D
E
F
U
V
3/4 x 5 1/2 x 96" Maple
C
C
D

Use business or playing cards as spacers to provide working clearance for the insert.

With the guide bearing of the pattern bit riding on the spacer strips and triangles, cut out the opening.

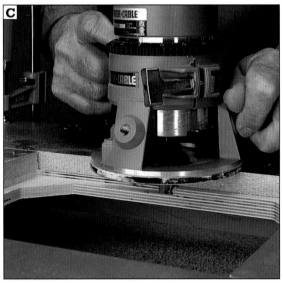

With the bearing of the pattern bit riding on the routing guides, form the insert recess.

Inserted from the front, the blanks for I and J make a snug fit between the base and the bottom of the table.

3 Place the insert on top of the routing guides and the router on top of the insert. Adjust the depth of cut so the pattern bit just grazes the exposed edge of the tabletop. Remove the insert, and rout the exposed lip of the tabletop, as shown in **Photo C.**

4 Round the corners of the insert plate to match the corners of the recess, and drill countersunk 3/16" holes, as shown in the Table Assembly drawing. Use the insert to mark the locations of the T-nut holes in the corners of the recess and drill the holes.

Complete the cabinet assembly

1 Mount the table assembly C/D/G between the sides of the cabinet assembly A/B. Insert studded knobs through the front holes in the cabinet sides, and screw them into the T-nuts at

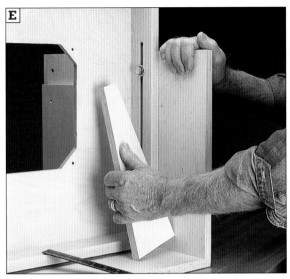

Working from the rear, square the table to the base, and position the braces.

Clamp the guides to the sides, inserting business cards for working clearance.

the front of the side skirts, as shown in the Table Assembly drawing. Insert hex bolts from the inside through the slots in the skirts and the rear holes in the cabinet sides. Secure the bolts with knobs.

2 Cut two 18 x 12¾" blanks for the braces (I) and table guides (J), and test them for a snug fit, as shown in **Photo D.** Trim the blank if necessary, then cut the braces and guides from the blanks, as shown in the Lift Mechanism drawing on *page 82.* To cut the rounded corners of the guides, make copies of the full-size pattern on *pages 174-175.* Adhere the patterns to the guide blanks with spray adhesive, and carefully jigsaw and sand the blanks to the pattern lines.

3 Remove the front studded knobs; loosen the rear knobs; slide the table back; and then, pivoting the table on the rear bolts, flip it vertically and lower it until it rests on the base. Square the table to the base and tighten the knobs. Position the braces (I) against the back of the table skirts, as shown in **Photo E.** Drill pilot and countersunk shank holes through the base (A) and sides (B) into the braces (I), and screw them in place.

4 Position the right table guide (J) against the inside of the cabinet, and push it back against the top of the table. Using the slot in the side (B) as a guide, mark the location of the slot on the table guide (J). Cut out the slot and drill the countersunk shank holes in both

guides (J). Now, pin the top between the braces in the rear and the guides in the front, as shown in the Parts View— Side drawing. Clamp the guides in place, as shown in **Photo F.** Using the pre-drilled shank holes as guides, drill pilot holes into the sides and firmly screw the table guides in place.

5 Return the table to its horizontal position, insert the front studded knobs, and tighten them. Check the size of the front opening and, allowing for a ¹⁄₁₆" gap all around, cut the doors (K) to size. Drill holes and install the pulls, as shown in the Cabinet Assembly drawing. Mount the hinges onto the doors and hang the doors on the cabinet. Install the magnetic catch. Remove the table and set it aside.

Create the lift mechanism

1 Form the arm block (L), as shown in the Lift Mechanism drawing. Position it inside the cabinet, centered beneath the slot in the right table guide (J), as shown. Drill pilot and countersunk shank holes through the base (A), side (B), and table guide (J) into the arm block, as shown on the Cabinet Assembly drawing on *page 78,* and screw the arm block in place.

2 Fasten two 8 x 13" blanks for the lift arms (M) together with double-faced tape. Make a copy of the lift arm pattern on the pattern insert, and adhere it to the blanks with spray adhesive. Drill the holes on your drill press, then bandsaw and sand the parts to the pattern line. Separate the parts and set them aside.

3 Cut a 2⅛" long piece of 1" dowel for the wrist pin (N). Using a V-block on your drill press, drill the counterbored hole, as shown on the Wrist Pin drawing (*above*). Epoxy one end of a ⅜" coupling nut into the counterbore and set the wrist pin aside.

Note: *The longer threaded length of a coupling nut spreads the stress of adjustment over more threads and reduces wear on both the nut and threaded rod.*

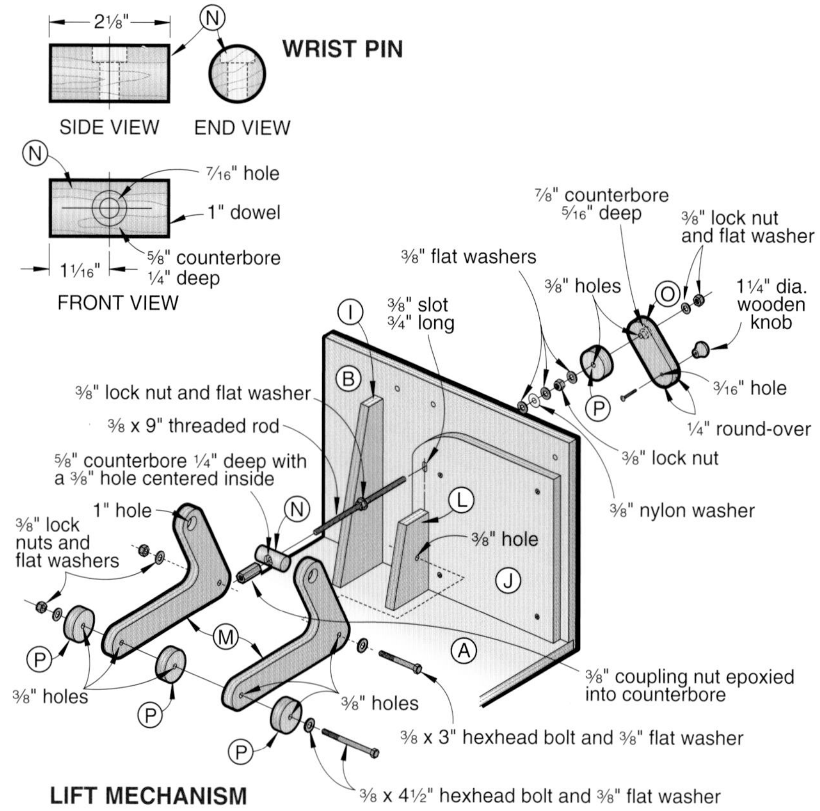
2⅛"
N
SIDE VIEW
END VIEW
N
7⁄16" hole
1" dowel
1 1⁄16"
⅝" counterbore
¼" deep
FRONT VIEW
⅞" counterbore
5⁄16" deep
⅜" lock nut
and flat washer
⅜" flat washers
⅜" holes
O
1¼" dia.
wooden
knob
I
⅜" slot
¾" long
B
⅜" lock nut and flat washer
⅜ x 9" threaded rod
⅝" counterbore ¼" deep with
a ⅜" hole centered inside
P
3⁄16" hole
¼" round-over
⅜" lock nut
⅜" nylon washer
1" hole
⅜" lock
nuts and
flat washers
N
L
⅜" hole
J
M
P
A
⅜" holes
P
⅜" holes
P
⅜" coupling nut epoxied
into counterbore
⅜ x 3" hexhead bolt and ⅜" flat washer
⅜ x 4½" hexhead bolt and ⅜" flat washer

WRIST PIN

LIFT MECHANISM

4 Make a copy of the crank (O) pattern on *pages 174-175*, and adhere it to a 2⅛ x 6½" blank. Drill the counterbore and holes, and bandsaw and sand the ends to shape. Rout the round-over on the edge of the counterbored face. Bandsaw four 2⅛" discs (P), drill ⅜" holes in their centers, and sand them to finish size.

Glue and clamp one of them to the back (no round-over) of the crank, aligning the ⅜" holes. Set the other discs aside. Glue and screw the wood knob to the crank.

5 Assemble the lift mechanism as shown *above,* using the three discs set aside in **Step 4.** With the crank and rod assembly protruding through the slot in the cabinet side, run the inside lock nut and washer up the threaded rod to the face of the table guide (J), allowing just enough play for the rod to swivel as the mechanism is adjusted up and down.

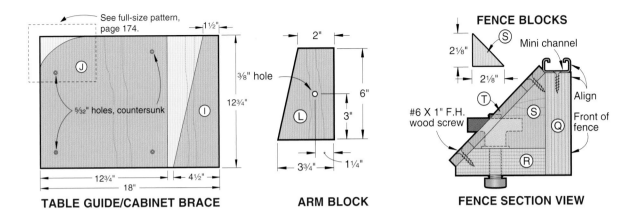

TABLE GUIDE/CABINET BRACE   **ARM BLOCK**   **FENCE SECTION VIEW**

Build your fence and a pair of stops

1 Cut the fence face (Q) to size. Use a dado blade in your tablesaw to cut the notch in two passes, as shown in the Fence Assembly drawing.

Tip: You can prevent unsightly tear-out by backing your cut with a wood auxiliary fence attached to your miter gauge.

Cut the fence base (R) to size. Rout the chamfer along the back edge, drill the holes, and form the semicircular cutout, as shown. Glue and clamp the fence face to the fence base, making sure they form a 90° angle.

2 Form the triangular fence blocks (S), as shown in the Fence Assembly drawing. Glue and clamp them to assembly Q/R as shown. Cut a length of mini-channel 24" long, and drill and countersink it for #6 flathead screws. Position it on the top edge of the fence,

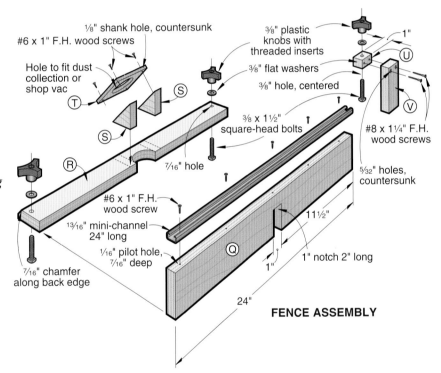

FENCE ASSEMBLY

with the front of the channel flush with the face of the fence. Drill pilot holes and screw the channel in place. Cut a 3¾ x 4" piece of ¼" hardboard for the vac port (T), and form a hole in it to fit your shop vacuum hose. Screw the vac port to the fence, as shown in the Fence Section View.

3 Cut the stop bases (U) and stopblocks (V) to size. Drill holes in the bases, as shown in the Fence Assembly drawing. Secure the bases to the channel with square head bolts and knobs. Position the stopblocks on the bases, using a square to align them so they are perpendicular to the length of the fence.

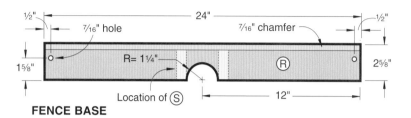

FENCE BASE

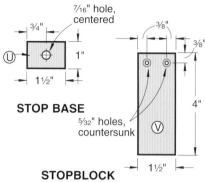

STOP BASE

STOPBLOCK

Clamp the stopblocks to the fence, and drill pilot and countersunk shank holes through the blocks and into the bases. Now, unclamp the blocks, apply glue, and drive the screws.

Finishing and final assembly

1 Remove the doors and door hardware. Disassemble the lift mechanism, leaving only the arm block (L) in place. Remove the bolts and knobs from the stops and the channel from the fence. Finish-sand all parts and assemblies to 220 grit. Apply two coats of satin polyurethane to the inside of the cabinet and all surfaces of the table, auxiliary table, lift arms, crank, rollers, fence, and stops. Sand between coats with 220-grit sandpaper.

2 Prime and paint the outside of the cabinet, including the edges of the base and sides, and all surfaces of the doors.

3 Reassemble the lift mechanism, greasing the threaded rod where the coupling nut runs. Mount the hinges and pulls, rehang the doors, and reinstall the magnetic catch. Cut two 11" lengths of channel, drill and countersink them for #6 flathead screws, and screw them to the top, as shown in the Table Assembly drawing. Install T-nuts in the corners of the insert recess. Screw the previously cut piece of channel to the fence.

4 Remove the subbase from your router, center it on the insert, and use it to mark the locations for the router mounting screws. Drill and countersink the holes, and mount the insert to the router. Chuck a ¼" brad-point drill bit in the router, and turning the collet by hand, mark a center point. Remove the router and drill a 1¼" hole in the insert. Remount the insert to the router, and then mount the combination in the top, fastening the insert into place with flathead machine screws.

5 Position the table in its vertical configuration by sliding it, front (T-nut end) first, into the slot between the braces and table guides and letting it rest on

the rear disc of the lift mechanism. Fasten it in place, through the slots in the side skirts, with hex head bolts, lock washers, flat washers, and knobs. Position the auxiliary table between the sides, resting on the table guides. Fasten it in place with four studded plastic knobs and washers.

6 Install square head bolts, washers, and knobs on the fence and stops, as shown in the Fence Assembly drawing. Slide the heads of the bolts in the stops into the channel on the fence and tighten the knobs. Next, slide the heads of the bolts in the fence into the channels on the table and tighten the knobs.

For an extra project that will make things even more convenient, you can build a leg stand for your new all-purpose router station. Just refer to the instructions on the *next page*.

SPECIAL FEATURE: A LEG STAND FOR STATIONARY TOOLS

A leg stand with tapered and slightly splayed legs makes a sturdy and attractive base for the all-purpose router station. In fact, it will also serve many other machines well, such as a portable planer.

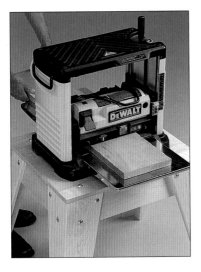

Use the dimensions shown in the Materials List *below* to make one for the router table, or alter the lengths of the parts and make one to fit a machine in your shop. To size the parts for any machine, follow these guidelines:

1. Subtract 1⅝" from the length of the machine for the length of the side rails (A).

2. Subtract 3¼" from the width of the machine for the length of the end rails (B).

3. Subtract 3" from the length of the side rails (A) for the length of the cleats (C).

4. Multiply your desired height by 1.074 for the length of the blanks for the leg halves (D).

Screw a piece of plywood to the cleats and bolt your machine to it.

Now, here's how to put your let stand together: After cutting the rails (A) and (B) to the dimensions shown on the Parts View drawing on *page 86,* screw them together to form a rectangular frame. Fit the cleats (C) into the rail frame and screw them in place. Set the frame aside.

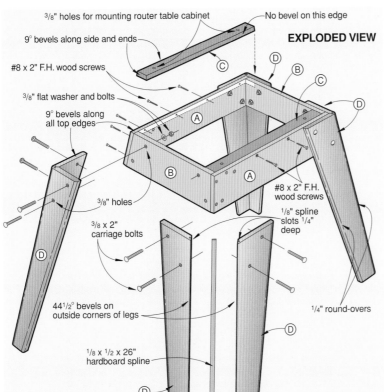

Materials List					
Part	**Finished Size**			Matl.	Qty.
	T	W	L		
A side rails	¾"	5"	25¼"	M	2
B end rails	¾"	5"	20"	M	2
C cleats	¾"	1½"	22¼"	M	2
D leg halves	¾"	6½"	27⅛"	M	8

Materials Key: M-maple
Supplies: ⅛" tempered hardboard, ⅜ x 2" carriage bolts, flat washers and nuts (16), #8 x 2" flathead wood screws (16), finish.

saw blade tilted at the same angle, cut spline slots in the bevels. Next, make the angled and beveled cuts at the top and bottom of each leg half. Do not cut the leg tapers until the halves have been glued together.

Clamp the frame upside down on your workbench. Apply glue to the mating bevels of the leg halves, and insert the splines. While holding the halves together by hand, clamp the legs to the frame. This will hold the halves at the proper angle while you finish clamping the length of the leg, as shown in the photo at *left*. When the

glue is dry, mark the tapers on the legs, and cut with a jigsaw or bandsaw. Clean up the cuts with a couple of passes over your jointer. Rout the round-overs, and using the holes drilled in the legs as guides, drill the holes in the frame.

Bolt the legs in place, and, if necessary, cut a piece of plywood and screw it to the cleats. Place your tool on the stand, and mark the locations of the mounting bolts with a pencil.

Drill the holes and apply the finish of your choice. When the finish is dry, bolt your machine in place and enjoy safe, rock-solid woodworking.

Cut blanks for the leg halves (D) to size, and before forming the legs, drill the holes where shown. Remember to make mirrored pairs. Bevel-rip the mating edges. Then, with the

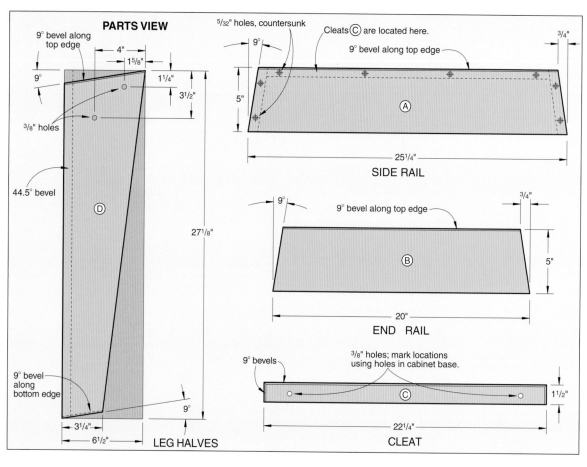

USING THE HORIZONTAL/VERTICAL ROUTER TABLE

You already know how useful your router can be with the bit pointed straight up or straight down. But imagine what feats you might accomplish using a bit in a horizontal position! Turned that way, your plunge router can handle several operations (raising panels, mortising, and tenoning, to name a few) much more easily and safely because the workpieces lie flat.

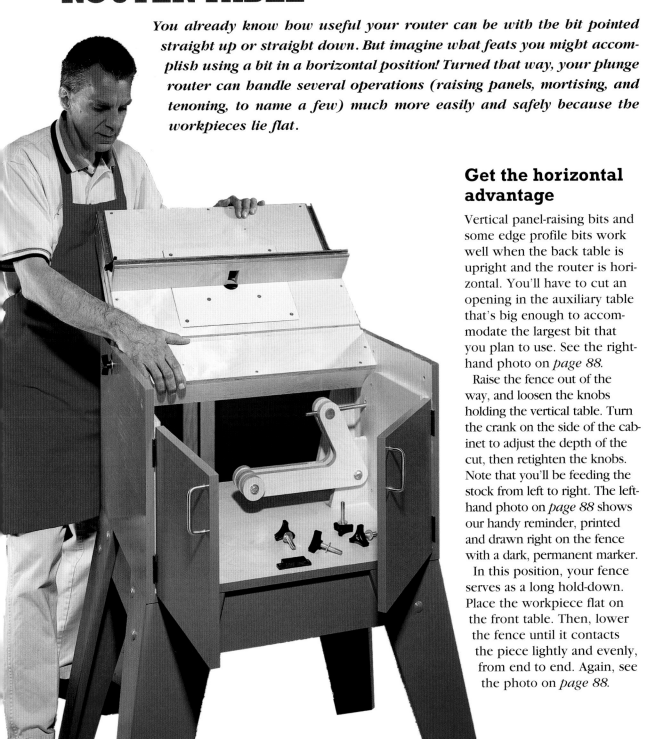

Get the horizontal advantage

Vertical panel-raising bits and some edge profile bits work well when the back table is upright and the router is horizontal. You'll have to cut an opening in the auxiliary table that's big enough to accommodate the largest bit that you plan to use. See the right-hand photo on *page 88*.

Raise the fence out of the way, and loosen the knobs holding the vertical table. Turn the crank on the side of the cabinet to adjust the depth of the cut, then retighten the knobs. Note that you'll be feeding the stock from left to right. The left-hand photo on *page 88* shows our handy reminder, printed and drawn right on the fence with a dark, permanent marker.

In this position, your fence serves as a long hold-down. Place the workpiece flat on the front table. Then, lower the fence until it contacts the piece lightly and evenly, from end to end. Again, see the photo on *page 88*.

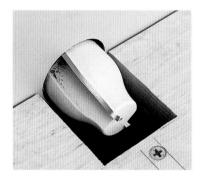

Only part of the bit extends above the work surface in the horizontal setup, so you'll have to cut an opening to accommodate the rest of it. We made ours 2" long and 1¾" wide, big enough to let this panel-raising bit spin freely.

Use the workpiece to set the fence as a hold-down. The stock must slide smoothly through from end to end for safety and a precise cut.

Make several light cuts to shape a profile, finishing up with a setting that just skims the surface (you'll get the smoothest possible result this way).

A hold-down block is yet another accessory you can build to use for mortise-and-tenon work at the end of a narrow board, or on the side of a narrow stile. See the drawing on *page 89* for dimensions and details. This will fit into the channel on the fence and keep your workpiece secure while providing a clear view.

An upcut spiral bit is great for mortise-and-tenon tasks. Install one in your router, use a couple of test pieces to

set the height and depth, and transfer your layout lines from the workpiece to the auxiliary table. When working on a short stile, use both stopblocks to control the cut (you'll be limited to one stopblock with longer workpieces). As shown in the right-hand photo on *page 89,* you can even cut into the end of a rail for loose tenons.

To form standard tenons, set the depth of cut, place the hold-down block in contact with the workpiece face, as shown in the left-hand photo on *page 89,* and cut the tenon's side shoulders in one or more passes. Use the miter gauge to support the workpiece. Loosen the fence

knobs and reset the height of the hold-down block when you flip the rail on edge to cut the final two shoulders.

Go vertical when necessary

Now let's say you want to reset the router to its vertical position so you can use a large-diameter panel-raising bit. Loosen the bolts that hold the auxiliary table in place and remove it. Loosen the bolts that hold the main table and crank the lift mechanism as low as it will go. Slide the table up and out of its slots, pivot it back and down, and fasten it with the knobs and bolts.

Slide the hold-down block into the fence channel, and center it whenever you need to keep a narrow piece in place for machining.

For mortising, set both stop blocks whenever possible. Guide the stock with your miter gauge.

Now you're back to the more familiar router table arrangement. Take advantage of the miter gauge slot to guide wide pieces with your tablesaw miter gauge. Use the stop blocks to make accurate stopped dadoes.

Remember, this design calls for a plunge router, and you must keep the plunge mechanism unlocked to adjust cutting height. The crank forces the router up along its plunge rods for a deeper cut (or lowers it for a lighter cut).

Make sure to tighten the knobs on the fence every time you reposition it. Feed the stock from right to left in this setup, and use a feather board when possible.

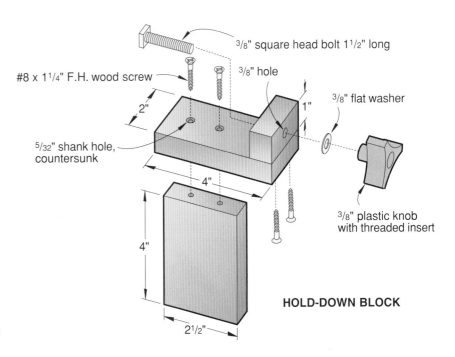

3/8" square head bolt 1 1/2" long

#8 x 1 1/4" F.H. wood screw

3/8" hole

2"

1"

3/8" flat washer

5/32" shank hole, countersunk

4"

3/8" plastic knob with threaded insert

4"

2 1/2"

HOLD-DOWN BLOCK

AN UPGRADE FOR YOUR ROUTER-TABLE FENCE

*This fence works perfectly with the router table extension project starting on **page 64**. However, it adapts to other situations as well because it can be clamped to any other fence. It's high (for vertical stability), has a pickup for dust collection, a right-angle support for joinery, and its guard and acrylic plate mean that the bit is always visible. In Chapter 4, you'll discover many of its uses.*

Prepare the pieces for the fence assembly

1 From ¾" plywood (birch will work well), cut the upright (A), base (B), clamping fence (C), and fence supports (D) to the sizes listed in the Materials List.

2 Transfer the dimensions from the Parts View drawing to the supports (D) and cut them to shape.

3 Mark the hole center-point on one support for a vacuum-hose opening. Clamp the support to your drill press table, and bore a hole in the support to accommodate your vacuum

hose (consider using a circle cutter, depending on your particular shop vac hose). You could also drill a blade-start hole, and cut the vacuum hole to shape with a scrollsaw or jigsaw.

Materials List

	Finished Size				
	T	W	L	Matl.	Qty.
FENCE ASSEMBLY					
A upright	¾"	5"	27"	BP	1
B base	¾"	5½"	27"	BP	1
C clamping fence	¾"	2½"	27"	BP	1
D supports	¾"	4"	5½"	BP	2
PUSHBLOCK					
E handle	1¹⁄₁₆"	3¼"	4½"	B	1
F base	¾"	5½"	7"	B	1
G fence	1¹⁄₁₆"	1"	8"	B	1
RIGHT-ANGLE SUPPORT					
H mounting plate	¼"	1¾"	5¼"	BP	1
I support	¾"	5¼"	7½"	BP	1
FEATHER BOARDS					
J long one	¾"	2⅜"	18"	B	1
K short one	¾"	2⅜"	8¾"	B	1
L support	¾"	¾"	9½"	B	1

Materials Key: BP–birch plywood, B-birch

Supplies: #8 x ¾" flathead wood screws, #8 x 1¼" flathead wood screws, #8 x 1½" flathead wood screws, 3–¼ x ¾" roundhead machine screws with 3–¼" flat washers and 3–¼" T-nuts, ½" dowel stock, ¼" acrylic for dust cover and guard, acrylic solvent cement, clear finish.

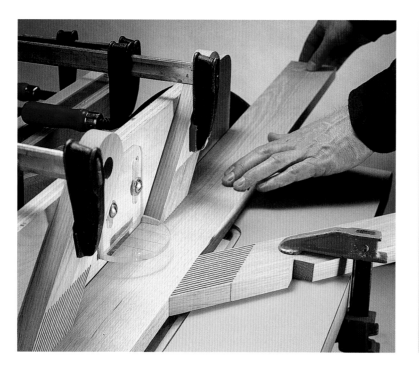

4 Using the Fence drawing for reference, mark the centerpoints and drill all the mounting holes in the upright (A). Don't forget to drill three ¾" counterbores ⅛" deep with a ⁵⁄₁₆" hole centered inside for the ¼" T-nuts.

5 Mark the location, and cut the 1¾ x 2" notch in the upright (A) and a ¾ x 2" notch in (B). Next, cut a ¹⁄₁₆ x ¹⁄₁₆" sawdust kerf along the bottom front edge of the upright.

6 Tap three ¼" T-nuts into their mating counterbored holes in the back surface of the upright (A).

7 Drill a 2" hole in the base for hanging when not in use.

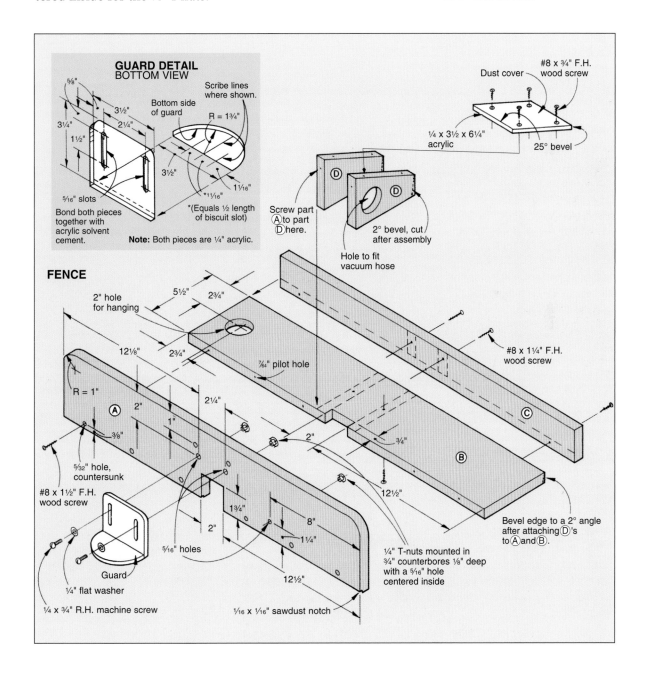

GUARD DETAIL
BOTTOM VIEW

⅝"
3½"
3¼"
2¼"
1½"
Bottom side of guard
Scribe lines where shown.
R = 1¾"
3½"
1¹⁄₁₆"
*11⁄₁₆"
⁵⁄₁₆" slots
Bond both pieces together with acrylic solvent cement.
*(Equals ½ length of biscuit slot)
Note: Both pieces are ¼" acrylic.

#8 x ¾" F.H. wood screw
Dust cover
¼ x 3½ x 6¼" acrylic
25° bevel

Screw part Ⓐ to part Ⓓ here.
2° bevel, cut after assembly
Hole to fit vacuum hose

FENCE

2" hole for hanging
5½"
2¾"
12⅛"
2¾"
⁷⁄₆₄" pilot hole
R = 1"
Ⓐ
2"
1"
2¼"
⅜"
⁵⁄₃₂" hole, countersunk
#8 x 1½" F.H. wood screw
2"
Guard
¼" flat washer
¼ x ¾" R.H. machine screw
1¾"
2"
⁵⁄₁₆" holes
8"
1¼"
¹⁄₁₆ x ¹⁄₁₆" sawdust notch
12½"
¾"
12½"
Ⓑ
Ⓒ
¼" T-nuts mounted in ¾" counterbores ⅛" deep with a ⁵⁄₁₆" hole centered inside
Bevel edge to a 2° angle after attaching Ⓓ's to Ⓐ and Ⓑ.
#8 x 1¼" F.H. wood screw

Assemble the fence

1 Clamp the upright to the base and use the previously drilled mounting holes in the upright to drill the pilot holes centered along the front edge of the base.

2 Glue and screw the upright to the base. Before the glue dries, glue and screw the supports (D) into place to keep the upright square to the base.

3 Tilt your tablesaw blade 2° from vertical, and raise it 2½" above the surface of the saw table. Bevel-cut the *back edge* of the base and supports. Bevel-cutting this edge at 2° ensures that the clamping fence (C) is positioned 2° from vertical after it is attached to the base/supports. When clamping the assembled fence to your tablesaw fence later, the bevel will cause the front edge of the fence to be held firmly against the router-table surface. This will prevent sawdust and chips from building up between the fence and table.

4 Drill the mounting holes, and glue and screw the clamping fence (C) to the back beveled edge of the fence assembly.

5 From ¼" acrylic, cut the dust cover to size, bevel-cutting or sanding the ends at a 25° angle, as shown on the Fence Drawing *(page 91)*.

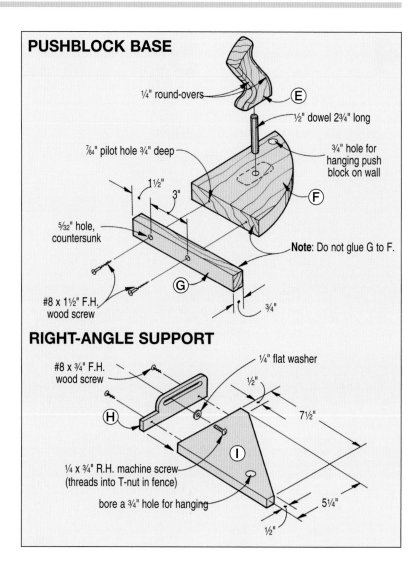

PUSHBLOCK BASE

¼" round-overs

E

½" dowel 2¾" long

⁷⁄₆₄" pilot hole ¾" deep

¾" hole for hanging push block on wall

1½"

3"

⁵⁄₃₂" hole, countersunk

F

Note: Do not glue G to F.

#8 x 1½" F.H. wood screw

G

¾"

RIGHT-ANGLE SUPPORT

#8 x ¾" F.H. wood screw

¼" flat washer

½"

H

7½"

¼ x ¾" R.H. machine screw (threads into T-nut in fence)

bore a ¾" hole for hanging

I

5¼"

½"

6 Drill and countersink mounting holes through the acrylic dust cover and into the top edge of each support (D).

Construct the pushblock

1 Cut the pushblock handle (E), base (F), and removable fence (G) to the sizes listed in the Materials List.

2 Enlarge and transfer the gridded patterns (E, F) from the Parts View drawing to the stock. Clamp the handle blank (E) in a handscrew clamp for support, and use a brad-point bit and your drill press to drill a ½" hole 2" deep in the bottom of the handle blank.

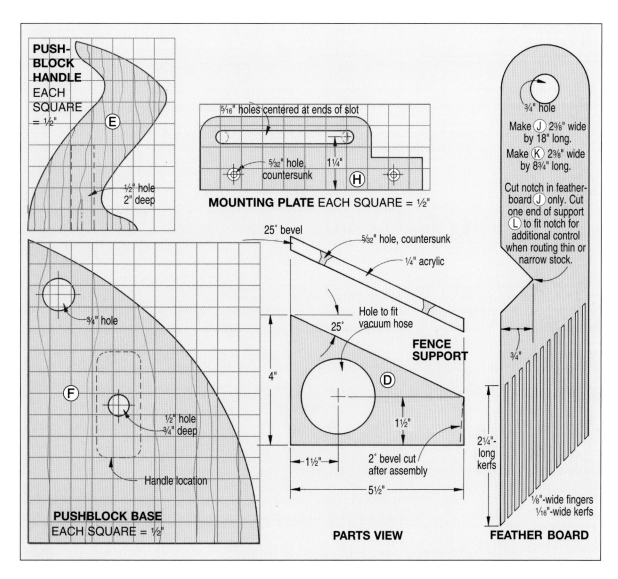

PUSH-BLOCK HANDLE EACH SQUARE = ½"

E

½" hole 2" deep

⁵⁄₁₆" holes centered at ends of slot

⁵⁄₃₂" hole, countersunk

1¼"

H

MOUNTING PLATE EACH SQUARE = ½"

¾" hole

Make J 2⅜" wide by 18" long.
Make K 2⅜" wide by 8¾" long.

Cut notch in feather-board J only. Cut one end of support L to fit notch for additional control when routing thin or narrow stock.

25° bevel

⁵⁄₃₂" hole, countersunk

¼" acrylic

Hole to fit vacuum hose

25°

FENCE SUPPORT

D

¾" hole

¾" hole

4"

½" hole ¾" deep

F

Handle location

1½"

2° bevel cut after assembly

5½"

1½"

2¼"-long kerfs

⅛"-wide fingers ¹⁄₁₆"-wide kerfs

PUSHBLOCK BASE EACH SQUARE = ½"

PARTS VIEW

FEATHER BOARD

3 Cut the pieces to shape and sand them smooth. Rout ¼" round-overs along the edges of the handle, as shown on the Pushblock drawing on *page 92*.

4 Bore a ½" and ¾" hole in the base, as shown on the Parts View drawing, *above*.

5 Cut a ½" dowel to 2¾" long. Glue and dowel the pushblock handle (E) to the base (F). Then, drill the mounting holes and screw (no glue) the fence (G) to the base. Because the router table fence piece is not glued in place, it will be easier to replace later, after you've routed into it numerous times.

Build the right-angle support

1 Cut the mounting plate (H) and support piece (I) to shape. See the Parts View drawing for the full-size pattern of part (H).

2 Drill a pair of ⁵⁄₁₆" holes in the mounting plates, and then cut the waste between the holes to form the slot, as shown in the Right-Angle Support drawing.

3 Drill the mounting holes, and glue and screw the two pieces together as shown.

4 Bore a ¾" hole in the support for hanging.

Add the guard and the finish

1 Using the Guard detail accompanying the Fence drawing for reference, cut the two guard pieces to shape from a piece of ¼" acrylic.

2 Draw the slot locations, as shown on the detail, and then drill a 5⁄16" hole at each end of each slot. (Because acrylic is hard to mark, apply masking tape onto the acrylic and mark the slot

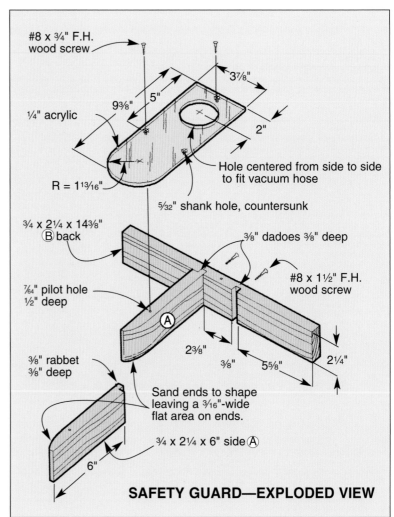

#8 x ¾" F.H. wood screw

3⅞"

5"

9⅜"

¼" acrylic

2"

Hole centered from side to side to fit vacuum hose

R = 1¹³⁄16"

5⁄32" shank hole, countersunk

¾ x 2¼ x 14⅜" Ⓑ back

3⁄8" dadoes 3⁄8" deep

#8 x 1½" F.H. wood screw

7⁄64" pilot hole ½" deep

Ⓐ

2⅜"

3⁄8"

5⅝"

2¼"

3⁄8" rabbet 3⁄8" deep

Sand ends to shape leaving a 3⁄16"-wide flat area on ends.

¾ x 2¼ x 6" side Ⓐ

6"

SAFETY GUARD—EXPLODED VIEW

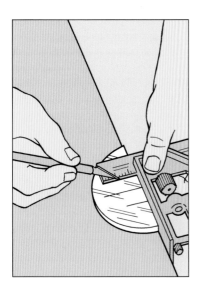

lines on the tape.) Scrollsaw the material between the holes to form the slots.

3 On the *bottom* face of the rounded piece of acrylic, scribe a center-line and two cutter end alignment lines on the acrylic. As shown in the illustration at *left*, consider using the *back* edge of an X-acto knife (it can be difficult to scribe a straight line using the cutting edge of a knife). The distance

between the alignment marks should be equal to the length of the biscuit slot cut with the biscuit cutter.

4 To make the scribed lines easier to see, high-light them with a marker.

5 Hold the pieces square-ly together, and use acrylic solvent cement to bond the two pieces of acrylic to finish forming the safety guard.

Time for the feather boards and finish

1 Using the Feather Board drawing for reference, cut one long and two short feather boards (J, K) and a feather board support (L) to size and shape.

2 Mark the locations and use your bandsaw to cut 1/16" kerfs (2¼" long each), as shown on the Feather Board drawing.

3 Mark the centerpoints, and bore a ¾" hole in the radiused end of

each feather board. You can use these holes later when hanging the feather boards between use.

4 Add a clear finish to all the wood parts. Later, attach the guard (*page 94*) to the upright (A) and the dust cover to the supports (D).

Add the safety guard

The fence shown here works really well for routing smooth, straight edges. For edges that curve gently, use the ends of the side pieces (A) as guide

pins for support when starting and stopping the cut. For an edge with more exaggerated curves, like the one shown *above*, move the guard back slightly and work directly off the piloted bit.

In addition to its basic uses, this guard will come in handy as a chip-collection hood. But most importantly, it will let you safely see your routing work without worrying about particles flying into your eyes.

4

Tricks at the Table

In chapter 3 you learned the benefits of mounting your router in a table. Now, with improved capability and accuracy, you'll be ready to tackle a whole host of woodworking tasks that you otherwise might not attempt. And yes, that even includes woodturning! This chapter highlights 12 expert tips and techniques that will help make the most of your newfound knowledge.

12 WAYS TO MAKE THE MOST OF YOUR ROUTER (AND TABLE!)

1 Good fences make good routing

Basically, a router-table fence consists of a straight piece of wood with a centered notch that surrounds the router bit. Like a tablesaw's fence, a router-table fence gives you a flat surface to guide a workpiece along. By adjusting the fence position, you can control the width of the cut. More sophisticated fences have built-in dust collectors and/or guards to help keep your fingers away from the spinning bit.

Router-table fences are a must for bits without pilot bearings, but its always a good idea to use a fence—even when routing straight workpieces with piloted bits. The fence minimizes the chances of kickback and prevents you from accidentally routing a portion of the workpiece's end grain when you only want to rout the edge.

To successfully use piloted bits with a router-table fence, you need to adjust the fence so the bit's bearing sits flush with the fence front or protrudes just beyond it, as shown at *left*. You can do this quickly by sighting along the length of the fence.

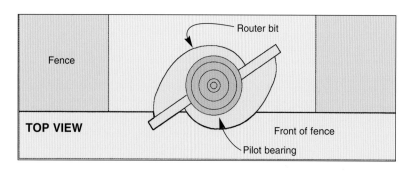

Fence

Router bit

TOP VIEW

Front of fence

Pilot bearing

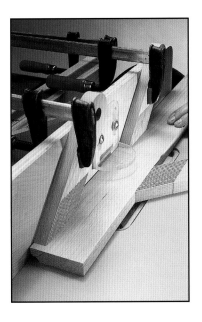

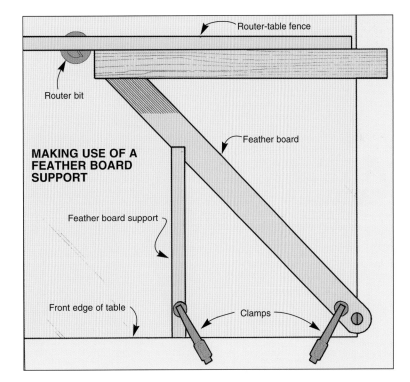

2 Feather boards

Feather boards will assist you in two ways. First, the angled, comb-like fingers prevent workpieces from kicking back; and second, feather boards help you rout consistently profiled edges.

As shown in the photo *above,* feather boards can hold workpieces firmly against the fence and table as you feed them. Without feather boards, it's hard to maintain consistent pressure on the workpiece near the bit, especially with stock measuring over 2' long.

To properly position feather boards, follow the procedure shown here. Be careful not to adjust the feather boards too tightly—this may slow down the rate of feed. If you have a deep router table—one where the bit sits more than 12" from the table's front edge— you should clamp on a ¾ × ¾" feather board support, as shown *above.* This will prevent the feather board from shifting.

3 Routing small moldings

For safety's sake, it pays to rout small moldings along the edge of a wide board, and then saw off the molding to its final size with a tablesaw. To cut down on waste, you often can rout two or four moldings from a single work-piece, as shown *below*.

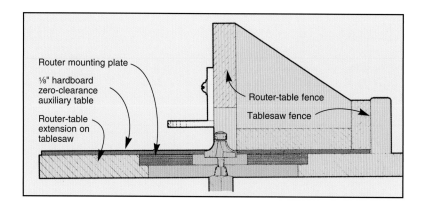

Router mounting plate

⅛" hardboard zero-clearance auxiliary table

Router-table extension on tablesaw

Router-table fence

Tablesaw fence

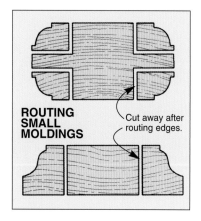

ROUTING SMALL MOLDINGS

Cut away after routing edges.

4 The zero-clearance table

Large-diameter router bits leave big holes in your router's mounting plate, and that's fine—until you try to rout small workpieces with small-diameter bits. Then, you will need a zero-clearance auxiliary table like the one shown at *top right*. It supports the workpiece fully so there's no danger of it tipping into the hole and catching an edge.

To make a zero-clearance auxiliary table, cut a piece of ⅛" hardboard to match the size of your router table, and drill a centered hole in it that's just slightly larger than your router bit's pilot bearing. Place the hole over the router bit, and clamp your fence onto the auxiliary table. Then, turn on the router and raise the bit through the auxiliary table to the desired height.

5 Using a push-block to tackle end-grain cuts

Because end-grain surfaces tend to be narrow, you may encounter lack of control or kickback as you try to pass them through the router bit. To help narrow workpieces safely bridge the gap in the

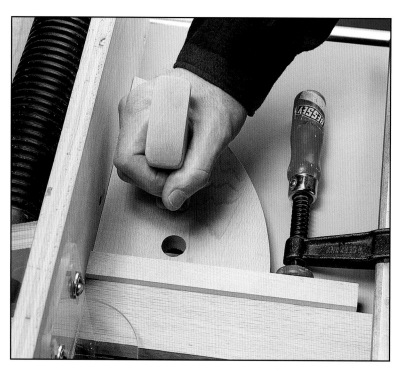

fence, you can use a push-block. By clamping your workpiece to the pushblock, as shown *opposite page (bottom)*, the workpiece will be held steady and square to the router bit as you slide the assembly along the fence.

When using a router bit with a pilot bearing, adjust the fence so that the bearing is flush with the fence or just barely protrudes from the fence as described earlier. As you use the pushblock, you'll inevitably remove some stock from the part of the pushblock closest to the fence. To save your pushblock and to prevent splintering on the exit edge of the workpiece, simply place a strip of ¾ × ¾" scrap between the pushblock and the workpiece.

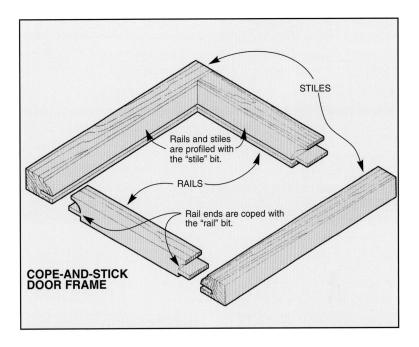

STILES

Rails and stiles are profiled with the "stile" bit.

RAILS

Rail ends are coped with the "rail" bit.

COPE-AND-STICK DOOR FRAME

6 Mastering rail-and-stile sets

With a set of these bits, you can make professional-quality cope-and-stick door frames, such as the one shown *at top right*. However, you need to know what to look for when buying a stile-and-rail router bit set, and how to make it work effectively.

There are several versions of these sets available, but you might want to start with rugged ½" shanks. And, if possible, go for a set that has a bearing between the profile cutter and the slotting cutter on the rail bit, as shown in the set *above*. Sets such as these

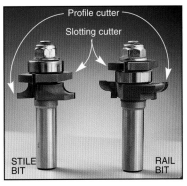

Profile cutter
Slotting cutter

STILE BIT   RAIL BIT

have thin shims between the cutters that may need to be adjusted, so it's a good idea to make your first cuts in scrap stock. When adjusted, the bits will produce rails and stiles that fit snugly together, with flush faces and profiles that align.

To make a door frame, start by adjusting the stile bit to the height that yields the desired profile. Although called a "stile" bit, this bit

cuts the visible profile on both the stiles *and* rails. The "rail" bit makes the coping cut on the ends of the rails.

Adjust your fence so the stile bit's pilot bearing is flush with the fence or barely protrudes from the fence. With the face side down, rout the profile along the inside edge of both stiles, as shown in the photo *above right*.

To cut coped rail ends, insert the rail bit and adjust its

Bottom of the rail bit's slotting cutter and edge of stile should align here.

RAIL BIT

STILE

height by holding a profiled stile edge up to it, as shown *above.* Again, adjust the fence so that the bit's bearing is flush with the fence or just barely protrudes from the fence. With the rails face side down and clamped to a push-block, make the coped cuts.

Finally, reinsert the stile bit, and profile the inside edges of the rails to match the profiled edge of the stiles. By saving this step for last rather than profiling the stiles and rails at the same time, you can clean up any splintering on the rails caused by the coping cuts. (For more details about stile-and-rail bits and their uses, see Chapter 6.)

7 When cutting curves, use a handy freehand guard

Like a fence, a freehand guard (see *page 94*) helps you safely feed workpieces into a router bit and collects wood shavings as you rout. But unlike a fence, a freehand guard, like

the one shown *below,* helps you rout curved workpieces and works only with router

bits that have pilot bearings. Here's how to use this invaluable helper.

After clamping the freehand guard to a fence, adjust it forward and back to accommodate your workpiece. To start a cut, hold the workpiece against the guard's starting point, and slowly pivot the workpiece into the bit. When the workpiece makes contact with the pilot bearing, remove the hand pressure against the starting point and rout the entire edge.

Starting point

8 Play it safe with a template

Let's say you want to make four table legs with matching curves. A table-mounted router and template will enable you to produce as many identical legs as you want.

Using ¼" hardboard or medium-density fiberboard, make a template to the shape you want. Use a bandsaw or scrollsaw to cut close to the line, then sand right up to it. Attach the template to your stock with cloth-backed, double-faced tape, orienting the grain for best effect. Bandsaw within ⅛" of the template all the way around.

Turning to your router table, you have two choices for router bits—a flush-trim bit or a pattern-cutting bit. (In some situations, you might need both.) A flush-trim bit has a ball-bearing pilot mounted at the tip. To use it, place your workpiece on the table with the template on top. Adjust the bit's height so the pilot runs on the edge of the template.

On pattern-cutting bits, the pilot sits between the shank

Cut the workpiece close to your template with a bandsaw before going to the router table. Trim bits are designed to handle light cuts only.

and the cutter. Your template rests on the table. Whichever bit you use, ease the workpiece into the bit until it contacts the pilot, then move the piece from right to left, as shown *above*. If you've left more than ⅛" of excess material in some spots, trim it to size with a couple of shallow passes. Don't pause too long in any spot or you'll burn the wood.

Double-check the surfaces you've just routed before removing the template.

Sometimes another pass will smooth out a rough spot. Finally, slide a putty knife blade between the workpiece and template, pop them apart, remove the tape, and you're done.

When you have a workpiece that's thicker than the cutting length of your bit, use a pattern-cutting bit and a flush-trim bit in sequence, as shown in Steps 1, 2, and 3, *below*. Make one pass with the pattern-cutting bit, template side down.

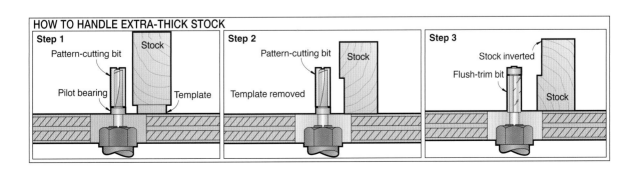

HOW TO HANDLE EXTRA-THICK STOCK

Step 1 — Pattern-cutting bit, Stock, Pilot bearing, Template

Step 2 — Pattern-cutting bit, Stock, Template removed

Step 3 — Stock inverted, Flush-trim bit, Stock

Remove the template, then make another pass with the pilot bearing riding on the surface you just machined. Finally, flip the workpiece over and use the flush-trim bit, with the pilot bearing riding on the previously milled surface.

9 Join up with biscuits

Biscuit joiners are great tools, but you also can do a lot of biscuit joinery right on your router table. All you need is a slot-cutting bit that matches the standard biscuit thickness of $5/32$" (see Chapter 5) and a miter gauge with an auxiliary fence attached.

Every time you set up to make a joint, center the cutter on the thickness of your stock, and make a test cut to double-check. To further reduce the risk of misalignment, mark the face of each component, then keep that side up.

Plunging a workpiece into a standard slot-cutting bit produces a slot that's shorter than a standard biscuit. You can lengthen the slot by moving the workpiece and making additional cuts. However, if you're going to make only a few joints, it's quicker and easier to shorten the biscuits. Here's how to cut slots for a rail-and-stile frame.

Use a steel rule to align the face of your router table fence with the front of the bit's pilot bearing. Place a piece of masking tape on the fence above

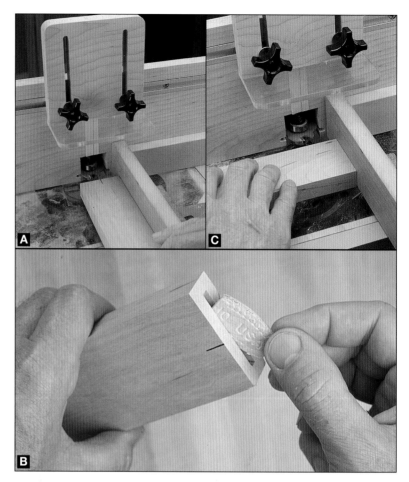

Photo A: Your miter gauge, backed by a stopblock, provides a solid, square guide as you push the end of a rail into the spinning slot-cutting bit.

Photo B: Trim the biscuit, slip it into the slot, and test the fit before gluing. If a gap shows, take a little more material off each end of the biscuit.

Photo C: Your setup remains the same when you cut a biscuit slot for a stile. This slot will perfectly match the slot in the previously milled rail

the bit. Then, use a square and a pencil to mark the center of the bit on the tape. Now, mark the center of a rail. Hold the length of the rail against your miter gauge, equipped with an auxiliary fence that nearly touches the router table fence, as shown in **Photo A**. Align the two center marks and clamp a stopblock on the router-table

fence so it meets the back of the miter-gauge fence. Using the miter-gauge fence as a support, plunge the workpiece squarely into the bit. Cut until it makes contact with the bearing.

Mark a biscuit at both ends, making each one slightly less than the slot length. Slice off the ends with a bandsaw. Test the fit (as shown in **Photo B**) to make sure that at least half of the biscuit's width slides into the slot.

To cut a matching slot on a stile, leave the miter gauge and stopblock in place. Carefully push the workpiece into the cutter, as shown in **Photo C**.

You can cut a slot in the other end of the stile with the same setup, but you have to flip the stock over, putting the face side down. If the slots are perfectly centered in the stock's thickness, that will work fine. The alternative is to measure the distance from the center of the bit to the miter gauge, then clamp a stopblock at that same distance to the left of the bit. Remove the miter gauge and right-hand stop from the router table, then cut a slot at the opposite end of the stile, still keeping the face side up.

We raised the guard for clarity in this photo. Keep it low while you're making dowels, to ensure that your fingers stay well away from the router bit.

10 Make really BIG dowels

Sometimes you need big dowels that match the wood of your project, but you won't find what you need at the store. To help you out, here's a simple router table technique.

You'll need a round-over bit with the same radius as the dowel's radius. For example, use a ½" round-over bit to make a 1" dowel. Chuck the bit in the router, and position the fence flush with the pilot bearing. Put two pieces of masking tape on the fence, one on either side of the bit, and mark two points 3" from the bit's center.

On the tablesaw, rip each dowel blank to a square profile equal in thickness to the desired diameter of the dowel. Crosscut it 6" longer than the finished dowel length.

Place your workpiece as shown in the drawing at *right*. Align the left end with the left-hand fence mark, as shown in the photo *above*, hold the end firmly against the fence, and begin routing any edge. Ease the workpiece into the bit, and move the blank across the bit until the right end reaches the right-hand mark. Repeat the procedure for each of the three remaining edges. The flat surfaces left at each end not only prevent the blank from rotating, but also keep your fingers at a safe distance from the bit.

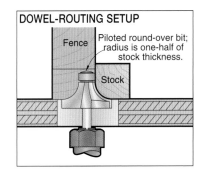

DOWEL-ROUTING SETUP

Fence

Piloted round-over bit; radius is one-half of stock thickness.

Stock

11 Keep it in line with a spline

Here's a handy method for beefing up long, mitered joints in jewelry boxes and the like. You can make slots for hidden splines with a straight bit, two stopblocks, and a simple support block.

Set your ⅛" straight bit to project ¼" above the router table. Clamp an auxiliary fence to your router-table fence, so that your workpiece won't slide into the bit-clearance notch. Set this fence the same distance from the bit's center as the thickness of your stock, or slightly farther. In the drawing *below*, we're cutting spline slots in ½"-thick pieces.

Miter-cut your box sides to length. Take the two ends of the box, or the front and the back, place them face-to-face, align the edges, and join them with cloth-backed, double-faced tape.

Bevel-rip a scrap piece at 45° to make a support board. Hold the taped-together assembly in the corner formed by the router table and fence, and use it to place the support

Cutting a spline slot is simple with this setup. Start at the right-hand stopblock, lower the workpiece onto the support guide, and slide it to the left stopblock.

board parallel to the fence. Clamp both ends of the support board to the router table.

Now, mark the ends of the planned slot on the workpiece. Use those marks, matched with the cutting edges of the bit, to set stopblocks on the fence to the left and right of the bit.

Turn on the router, hold the workpiece firmly against the fence, and lower it onto the spinning bit, as shown in the photo *above*. Keep the right side of the workpiece

against the right-hand stopblock. Carefully slide the workpiece across the table to the left-hand stopblock, and raise it straight up the fence.

After cutting eight slots for a rectangular box, cut matching splines. Hardboard and plywood work really well for this, or you can cut splines from the same wood used for the box. In that case, the grain of the splines should run in the same direction as the sides to avoid problems with wood movement.

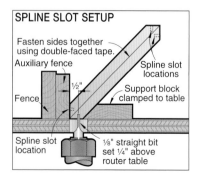

SPLINE SLOT SETUP

Fasten sides together using double-faced tape.
Auxiliary fence
Spline slot locations
Fence
½"
Support block clamped to table
Spline slot location
⅛" straight bit set ¼" above router table

12 Make your router a joiner

You can equip your table with a split fence for edge-jointing, or you can take the low-tech route shown here. We simply clamped a piece of plastic laminate on the outfeed (left-hand) side of the fence. Use sandpaper to ease the edge nearest the router bit, so it won't catch your workpiece as the board slides past. As seen in the photograph at *right*, a steel rule was used to align the laminate with the cutting edge of a straight bit mounted in the router.

Set the bit high enough to trim the entire edge of the board in one pass. Then, turn on the router, and move the board across the table from right to left. You'll remove ¹⁄₁₆"

Laminate piece

Place your laminate piece at the left-hand edge of the bit-clearance notch in the router table fence. The solid backing will keep it from flexing.

with each pass, and leave a perfectly straight, square edge. Repeat the procedure with a second board, and the two pieces can be glued together without any gaps!

SHOP TIP *Set your table with custom plates*

Router table work goes smoother and more safely when the hole in your insert plate is only slightly larger than the diameter of the bit. You can buy a plate with removable rings, which gets you close enough in most situations—or you can make a custom plate to match a bit exactly. Use Baltic birch plywood for the least expensive plate, or choose polycarbonate for a clear plastic plate. You can buy a 12 x 12" piece of ⅜" polycarbonate for about $15–$20.

Place the insert plate faceup on a flat surface. Remove the sub-base from your router, and adhere it to the plate, faceup, with double-faced tape. Be sure it's centered, and oriented so that your router will be convenient to operate once it's mounted under the table. Select a drill bit the same size as the holes in the subbase, and chuck it in your drill press. Using the holes in the subbase as guides, drill matching holes through the insert plate. Remove the subbase, and countersink the holes.

Now, attach the insert plate to your unplugged router and set it flat on your workbench. Chuck a ¼" drill bit in the router, and lower it until the bit touches the insert plate. Turn the collet by hand to mark the centerpoint.

Remove the insert plate from the router. Chuck a holesaw or adjustable circle cutter in your drill press to cut a center hole of the diameter needed, as shown here.

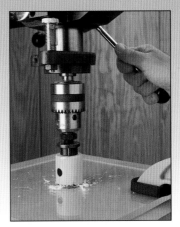

Clamp your insert-plate blank and a backer board to your drill-press table, centered under the bit of your holesaw. Drill slowly, and you'll get a clean cut.

ROUTER TABLE WOODTURNING

No lathe? No problem. Believe it or not, you can rotate stock over a spinning bit to make tapered table legs as well as other decorative cuts. And don't be intimidated—it's actually fairly easy.

You'll need a simple fence system

To get things underway, build the router-table fence, stops, and dust-collection accessory shown at *right*. The 6"-high fence works with turnings that have round or multi-sided discs up to 12" in diameter. These discs mount to the ends of the workpiece and support it as you slide or rotate the workpiece along the fence as shown *opposite*.

Discs: the key ingredient

Just as lathe-turned work-pieces rotate against a cutter as they take on a rounded shape, so do router-turned objects. The low-tech solution for rotating router-turned objects: round wooden discs screwed on center to both ends of the workpiece.

To make the discs, first measure diagonally (corner to opposite corner) on the end grain of your workpiece. Add ¼" to this measurement, and with a compass draw a circle of this diameter onto a piece of ¾"-thick stock. Bandsaw the disc roughly to shape, staying just outside the marked line. Drill a ⅛" hole through the center of the disc.

For router-table turning to work well, you must create perfect circles. Fortunately, this is easy to do. Simply make a disc-sanding jig like the one shown at *right*. Place the hole of the disc

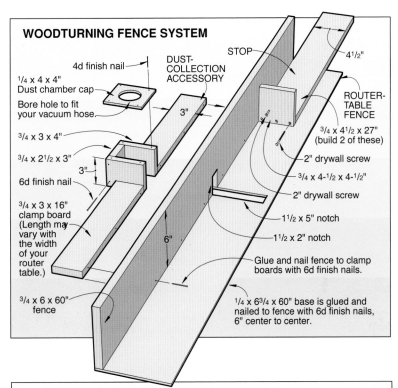

WOODTURNING FENCE SYSTEM

- 4d finish nail
- DUST-COLLECTION ACCESSORY
- STOP
- 4½"
- ¼ x 4 x 4" Dust chamber cap
- Bore hole to fit your vacuum hose.
- 3"
- ROUTER-TABLE FENCE
- ¾ x 3 x 4"
- ¾ x 4½ x 27" (build 2 of these)
- ¾ x 2½ x 3"
- 2" drywall screw
- 3"
- ¾ x 4-½ x 4-½"
- 6d finish nail
- 2" drywall screw
- ¾ x 3 x 16" clamp board (Length may vary with the width of your router table.)
- 6"
- 1½ x 5" notch
- 1½ x 2" notch
- Glue and nail fence to clamp boards with 6d finish nails.
- ¾ x 6 x 60" fence
- ¼ x 6¾ x 60" base is glued and nailed to fence with 6d finish nails, 6" center to center.

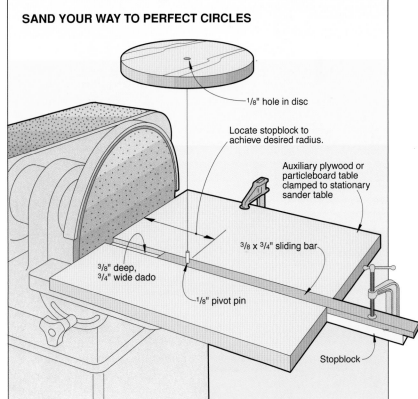

SAND YOUR WAY TO PERFECT CIRCLES

- ⅛" hole in disc
- Locate stopblock to achieve desired radius.
- Auxiliary plywood or particleboard table clamped to stationary sander table
- ⅜ x ¾" sliding bar
- ⅜" deep, ¾" wide dado
- ⅛" pivot pin
- Stopblock

A Few More Things You'll Need

To get off on the right foot, we advise you to draw a rough sketch of how you would like your finished project to appear. The drawing at *bottom* shows a sketch of the workpiece we produced for this project. Note the names of the leg's various features.

Depending on the complexity of your design, you'll need one or more router bits to execute various cuts. The drawings *below* show some of the basic bits for router turning. How you use each one will become clear in the following sections.

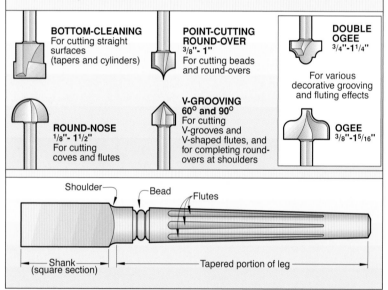

BOTTOM-CLEANING For cutting straight surfaces (tapers and cylinders)

POINT-CUTTING ROUND-OVER 3/8"- 1" For cutting beads and round-overs

DOUBLE OGEE 3/4"-1 1/4" For various decorative grooving and fluting effects

ROUND-NOSE 1/8"- 1 1/2" For cutting coves and flutes

V-GROOVING 60° and 90° For cutting V-grooves and V-shaped flutes, and for completing round-overs at shoulders

OGEE 3/8"-1 5/16"

Shoulder — Bead — Flutes

Shank (square section) — Tapered portion of leg

face-planing bit) produces an even smoother cut.

Note: *No matter what cut you make, remember to always center the router bit directly under the workpiece.*

To make your first cut, turn the router on and slowly lower the left end of the workpiece onto the router bit (with the right-side disc in contact with the stop screw on the right-side stop). Move the workpiece from right to left until you contact the left-side stop. Without rotating the stock, slide it back to the right. Now, rotate the bottom of the workpiece toward the fence about 1/2" and make another cut from right to left. Repeat this procedure until you have cut the entire workpiece to a consistent diameter. Keep in mind

POSITIONING THE WORKPIECE, FENCE, AND STOPS

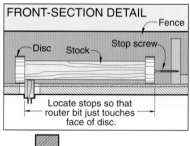

FRONT-SECTION DETAIL — Fence
Disc Stock Stop screw
Locate stops so that router bit just touches face of disc.

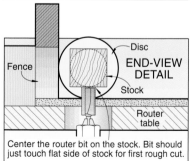

Fence — Disc
END-VIEW DETAIL
Stock
Router table
Center the router bit on the stock. Bit should just touch flat side of stock for first rough cut.

onto the pivot pin and slowly advance the disc into the sander. Set the stopblock when the sanding surface removes stock up to the compass-made layout line. Slowly rotate the wheel to make it circular.

Try your hand at a simple cylinder

After drawing diagonal lines on the ends of your work-piece, mark the centerpoint of each with an awl. Then, center and fasten a disc to each end of your workpiece with 1 1/2" drywall screws as shown on *page 111*. Check to make sure that no part of your workpiece extends past the rims of the discs.

Now, position your workpiece, fence, and stops as shown *right*. A straight bit works for this task, but we found that a bottom-cleaning bit (also referred to as a sur-

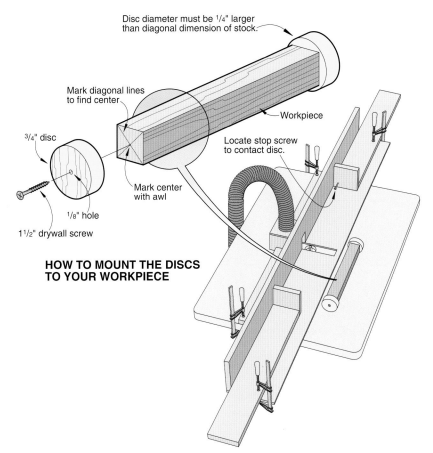

Disc diameter must be 1/4" larger than diagonal dimension of stock.

Mark diagonal lines to find center

Workpiece

3/4" disc

Locate stop screw to contact disc.

Mark center with awl

1/8" hole

1 1/2" drywall screw

HOW TO MOUNT THE DISCS TO YOUR WORKPIECE

that you'll get a smoother surface by rotating the workpiece in small increments.

You can reduce the diameter further by raising the router bit 1/8–1/4" and repeating this process. These relatively deep cuts may leave a slightly rough surface, so remove only 1/16" or so of stock on your last series of cuts.

These simple changes will help you produce a tapered leg

First, mount discs of equal size to your workpiece just as described earlier for making cylinders. With a round-nose bit, cut a groove that defines the area where the top of the taper meets the shoulder, as shown *below left.* Make these cuts in several passes, remembering to always rotate the

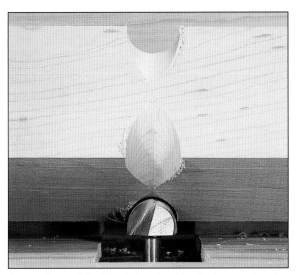

A round-nose bit will cut the shoulder that separates the shank from the tapered portion. Make the cut in several light passes to avoid splintering.

Although straight bits also work, bottom-cleaning bits like this one work best for cutting flat surfaces from the shank to the shoulder.

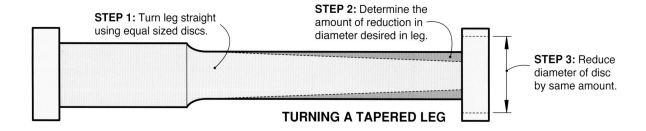

STEP 1: Turn leg straight using equal sized discs.

STEP 2: Determine the amount of reduction in diameter desired in leg.

STEP 3: Reduce diameter of disc by same amount.

TURNING A TAPERED LEG

Using discs of different sizes, you can create tapered workpieces.

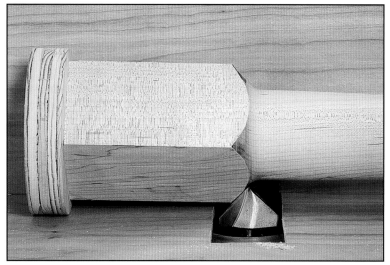

V-grooving bits cut a smooth transition from the shank to the shoulder.

bottom of the workpiece into the fence.

Switch to a bottom-cleaning bit, readjust the stops, and turn the leg to a cylinder, as shown in Step 1 of the drawing *above*. Cut the cylinder no deeper than the bottom of the rounded groove at the base of the shoulder. Follow Steps 2 and 3 of the same drawing to determine the size of the smaller disc at the narrow end of the taper. Mount the smaller disc and taper the leg using the same method for making a cylinder.

Finally, use a V-grooving bit to smooth the transition from the shoulder to the shank, as shown in the photo at *bottom left*. Take light, controlled cuts to prevent grain tear-out and chipping.

Follow these steps for great-looking beads

To cut beads, you need a point-cutting round-over bit, generally available in $\frac{3}{8}$–1" diameters. Your beads will look perfect as long as you space them accurately.

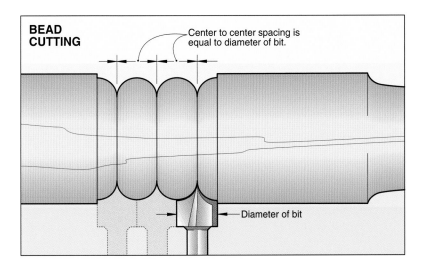

BEAD CUTTING

Center to center spacing is equal to diameter of bit.

Diameter of bit

As shown *above,* the diameter of the bit determines the center-to-center bead spacing. After deciding how many beads you would like on your project, simply transfer spacing marks to your router-fence base, as shown at *bottom left.* These marks tell you how far to advance your right-hand stop for each successive beading cut. Once the right-hand stop is set, snug the left-hand stop so that the stopscrew touches the disc.

Adjust the router bit so it makes a full cut. Turn the router on and hold the left-hand wheel above the router table as you set the right-hand wheel against the right stop. Slowly lower the workpiece onto the router bit to start the cut, and rotate the stock to complete the beading cut. Before making the next cut,

advance the right-hand stop up to the next spacing mark, readjust the left stop, and make your second cut, as shown at *bottom right.*

Add a classical touch with flutes

By replacing the discs on both ends of your workpiece with flat-sided shapes, such as hexagons, you can rout flutes into the cylindrical or tapered sections of your project. On a cylindrical workpiece the flutes will be a consistent depth over their entire length. But on tapered legs, the flutes will decrease in depth over the length of the leg until they disappear, as shown in the opening photo of this section.

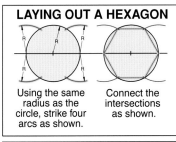

LAYING OUT A HEXAGON

Using the same radius as the circle, strike four arcs as shown.

Connect the intersections as shown.

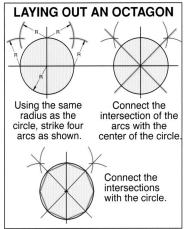

LAYING OUT AN OCTAGON

Using the same radius as the circle, strike four arcs as shown.

Connect the intersection of the arcs with the center of the circle.

Connect the intersections with the circle.

Mark the bead spacing on the base of the router-turning fence.

Point-cutting round-over bits produce perfectly shaped beads.

Discs with flat edges (in this case, six) will help you cut evenly spaced flutes of varying numbers.

The number of flutes will be the same as the number of flat surfaces on the shapes you attach to the ends of the workpiece. For example, hexagon ends will help you produce workpieces with six evenly spaced flutes. The drawings on *page 113* will help you lay out hexagon and octagon discs. After cutting the shapes from ¾" stock, attach them with drywall screws so that the flat surfaces align with each other.

Note: *You must exactly center the discs on the workpieces. Otherwise, your flutes will not be consistent in depth.*

To align the flat surfaces of the shapes, set the workpiece on a flat surface as you tighten the screws, as shown *above.* Then, add an off-center screw to each end to keep the multi-sided ends from rotating.

To cut the flutes, set your stops for the length and positioning of the flutes on the workpiece. Hold the left end of the workpiece above the router table, and place the right-hand shape against the right-hand stop with a flat side of the shape lying flat on the router table. Lower the left end of the workpiece onto the router bit and feed the stock from right to left.

Lift the workpiece up after you cut each flute, rotate it for the next cut, and repeat this procedure.

Final touches

Although your flutes and beads should come out pretty smooth, you'll have to sand the cylindrical and tapered portions of your workpieces. We suggest you remove small ridges and wood-grain fuzz with 80- or 100-grit sandpaper. Do the final smoothing work through a succession of 150- and 220-grit abrasives.

shopTIP

Woodturning for bigger workpieces

If necessary, you can apply the woodturning techniques discussed in this article to large objects, such as pedestal columns—you just need to make a few accommodations. For long projects you will need to lengthen the fence. For large-diameter workpieces composed of staves, you attach discs, as shown here.

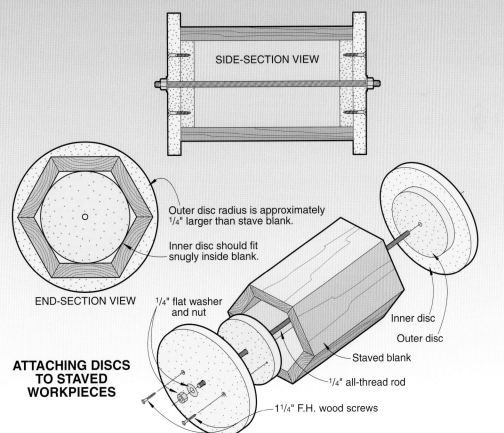

SIDE-SECTION VIEW

Outer disc radius is approximately ¼" larger than stave blank.

Inner disc should fit snugly inside blank.

END-SECTION VIEW

ATTACHING DISCS TO STAVED WORKPIECES

¼" flat washer and nut

Inner disc

Outer disc

Staved blank

¼" all-thread rod

1¼" F.H. wood screws

5 Selecting Router Bits

*S*ome woodworkers will tell you that their router-bit collections seem to grow while they're not looking, as if guided by a mysterious power. But the truth is, each particular bit usually is bought for the job at hand. Thus, the more jobs you attempt, the more bits you'll collect. This chapter will introduce you to the all-important router bit and provide you with a basic explanation of what they do. This will help you save money while obtaining the best possible tool combinations for your projects.

Reading a router-bit catalog can make you feel like the proverbial "kid in a candy store." With literally hundreds of styles available, choosing the right size, shape, or material can be overwhelming. So, start with the basics.

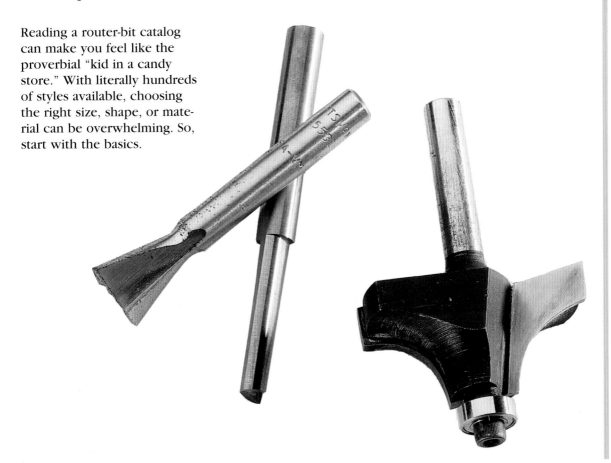

WHAT YOU NEED TO KNOW

Design

All router bits share certain design similarities. Each one has a continuous steel body and shank made from one piece of steel and one or more cutting edges. The cutting edges are made from either high-speed steel (HSS) or brazed tungsten carbide tips.

Today, more and more bits are being made on automatic lathes and computer-driven multi-axis grinding machines. These machines do a good job, and also enable the manufacturers to produce designs that were not possible to make just a few years ago. In addition, some very complex bits are now being made by investment casting. Their cutting edges will be either HSS or tunsten carbide.

Refer to the bit anatomy drawing on *page 119* to identify those parts you may not be familiar with.

Shank size

Shank size should always be your first consideration when buying a router bit. Routers can have either ¼" or ½" collets—sometimes both. A ¼" collet will only accept bits with ¼"-diameter shanks. A ½" collet will accept bits with ½"-diameter shanks and, with adapters, also ¼" and ⅜" bits (not widely available). If you plan to use your router frequently, it's nice to have one that accepts both shank sizes. However, a router with a specific shank size won't put much of a limit on what you can do—many types of bits are available in both ¼" and ½" shank sizes.

Although bits with ¼" shanks perform well, many experienced woodworkers prefer ½" shank bits because they're bigger, stiffer, stronger, and are better able to resist vibration, flexing, and breaking.

Consider shank length, too. As a general rule, try to pick the bit with the shortest shank that will do the job effectively.

Caution: Some users have experienced problems with bargain bits due to undersized shanks and low-quality metals. If you plan to buy bits from an unknown source, check them closely first.

Bit dimensions

Router bits have several critical dimensions. Besides shank diameter and length, you need to know the cutter diameter, cutter height (or length), cutter width, and overall bit length. On some,

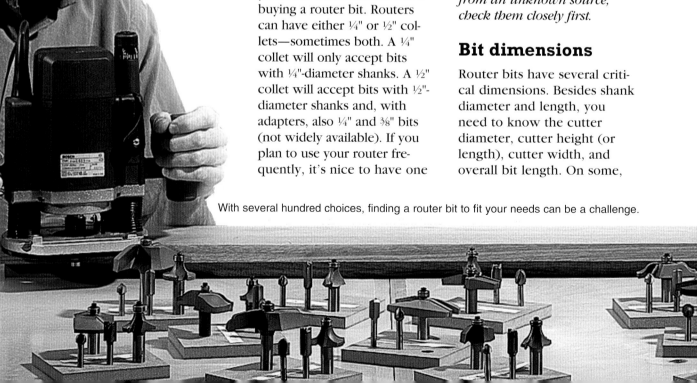

With several hundred choices, finding a router bit to fit your needs can be a challenge.

the cutter angle, radius, or bearing diameter also will be important. Profiles of bits and illustrations showing an exact image of the cut also help in visualizing what the final cut will look like.

The cutting edge: carbide or high-speed steel?

Most manufacturers now use tungsten carbide for the cutting edges. Carbide is an alloy of carbon and metal powders fused together, and harder than HSS. Carbide tips hold a cutting edge anywhere from 15 to 25 times longer. If you plan to work hardwoods or any manmade products, such as MDF or Corian, buy carbide-tipped bits.

HSS bits cost about half as much as good carbide bits. They can be sharpened to a keener edge than carbide, and some manufacturers coat them with a titanium alloy to make them more durable and stay sharp longer. But HSS is softer than carbide, and the cutting edges dull fast when working with abrasive materials. Carbide bits, even though the edges are prone to chipping and nicking, stay sharp longer, and can be sharpened many more times. You should find

the extra money for quality carbide bits well spent.

To pilot or not to pilot

Unguided bits can be used for straight or contour cuts anywhere on a board, provided the router is guided by a straightedge or template. Guided bits have a pilot or bearing that controls the router without the aid of a straightedge. They can only be used along the edge of a board.

Most edge-cutting bits use ball bearings, typically located at the end of the shank on edge-forming bits, to ride against the workpiece edge. To eliminate edge burn, the bearings turn at your feed rate on the outside, but spin at router speed on the inside. You must put enough pressure on the router to hold the bearing against the workpiece. Otherwise, it may spin along with the bit, and at this speed, will burn the wood.

Changing the bearing diameter will alter the cutting width and profile of the bit, which in effect, gives you several bits in one. To change a bearing requires removing the socket-head cap screw located on the end of the shank with an Allen wrench.

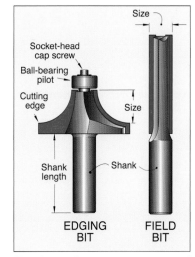

Bits have key components and dimensions that help identify them. Dimensions reference overall length; shank diameter and length; cutter length and width or diameter; and, on some bits, the cutter's angle or radius and bearing diameter.

Many woodworkers use changeable bearings on rabbeting bits and slot cutters to change the rabbet's width or the slot's depth. Fitting a round-over bit with a smaller bearing converts it into a beading bit. The profiles of certain classical bits can be altered in this way too.

On pattern-cutting bits, the bearing is located above the cutter. In use, the bearing follows along the edge of the pattern or template, and the cutter duplicates the pattern's profile on the workpiece. You can buy bearing kits to convert certain non-piloted, edge cutting bits into pattern-cutting bits. Just slip the bearing and stop collar over the bit's shank, and tighten the set screw in the collar.

SPECIAL FEATURE: ROUTER BIT VOCABULARY

Arbor: The part of the bit inserted into the router collet. On an assembled bit, the lower part of the arbor also holds the cutter and pilot tip. It may also be referred to as the *shank.*

Assembled bit: A bit made up of several pieces. The arbor usually accommodates interchangeable cutters and pilot tips; also called an *interchangeable arbor.*

Carbide tip: A tungsten carbide alloy brazed to a router bit's cutting edge to increase bit life.

Cutting face: The cutting part of the bit, which can be either straight or angular (up-shear).

Flute: The opening in front of the cutting edge of a bit that provides clearance for the wood chips. Bits may have one or more flutes, and they may be straight, angular, or spiral. Flutes are also referred to as *chip pockets or gullets.*

Hook angle: The angle of the cutting face in reference to the center line of the bit. Hook angle affects feed rate and bit control.

Pilot tip: The noncutting portion of a bit that limits the cut and guides the path of the bit by running along the edge of the work. A pilot tip may be a ball bearing or a solid piece of steel.

Radial relief: The clearance angle behind the cutting edge on the periphery of the bit that keeps the bit from rubbing on the work.

Solid bit: A bit machined out of a single piece of tool steel. In some cases, a ball bearing pilot tip is fastened to it. Solid, or one-piece, bits usually have closer machining tolerance than assembled bits.

Stagger-tooth bit: A bit on which the cutting edges do not extend the complete length of the flute.

Up-shear: Another term for the inclined cutting face on a bit. The angle of the cutting face shears the chip in an upward fashion.

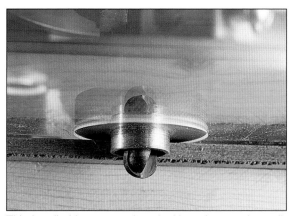

This handheld router equipped with a shop-made auxiliary base, template guide bushing, and core-box bit is ready to tackle a template-routing task. Note that the operator is using the outside edge of the template to set bit cutting depth.

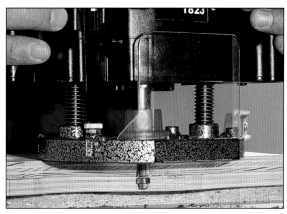

A bearing on this flush-trimming bit guides along the pattern edge, and cuts an identical edge on the piece above it. This setup is an excellent way to make finish-quality, duplicate workpieces quickly, easily and without any additional work.

Bit quality: What to look for

Not all bits are created equally—not even carbide bits. While carbide might be the all-around best, there will still be differences—in carbide thickness, grades of carbide used, and how the bit's body supports the carbide. The naked eye can see some of the things that make up quality, but not all of them.

For example, you can spot a skinny carbide tip that will likely disappear after just a few sharpenings. But when it comes to the grade of carbide used, you have no way of knowing what the manufacturer used. Very hard carbide maintains a sharp edge longer. But if it's too hard, the cutting edge may chip or nick more easily.

Carbide tips get brazed to the bit body during manufacturing. How well this is done depends on the welder's skill.

Tips also should be fully supported by the bit body to minimize chances of the carbide breaking away. The steel body should be turned smooth and without pits or cracks.

Check the edge grind of the carbide tip under a good magnifying glass if possible—it should be glassy smooth. If you see or can feel grinding marks, the tips have not been finished properly and the bit should be rejected. Other design elements, such as the flute, rake angle, and clearance angle, belong in the domain of the design engineer. They are part of what makes a bit work—and why some work better for certain routing applications than others.

Bits must also be rounded and balanced. If not, they'll vibrate while spinning in the router. If you have a dial indicator or gauge, mount each new bit in the router collet and measure how much they

deviate from a perfectly concentric orbit (runout). Any measurement less than .003" is acceptable.

Anti-kickback design for safety

Anti-kickback bits provide an extra margin of safety. The design limits the depth of cut at each pass to about ¹⁄₁₆". Limiting the bite is especially beneficial on large-diameter

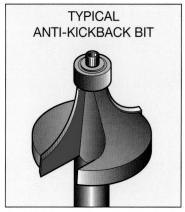

TYPICAL
ANTI-KICKBACK BIT

Anti-kickback bits have a body shaped to limit bite.

bits that take wide cuts because it lessens the risk of the bit grabbing or throwing a workpiece. Their additional body mass also helps dissipate heat quicker, and it sometimes seems to make them run smoother.

How to spot a multi-axis grind

The distinction between a fixed-axis grind and a multi-axis grind, although subtle, can be very important when cutting certain stock. The drawings *below* show that the relief angle on a multi-axis grind bit stays consistent across the full length of the grind. This enables the bit to deliver a slightly better quality cut than the fixed-grind bit.

Differences between straight and shear flute cutters can be critical too. On a straight flute bit, the entire cutting edge contacts the work at the same time. By contrast, on a spiral flute, only a small portion of the cutting edge contacts the work at any given time. This shearing action makes a smoother, finer finished cut with less

power. Although this feature appears most evident on straight bits, you also can find spiral shear flutes on other high-quality bit profiles.

Spiral-cutting bits make fast, clean cuts because they move chips out of the way quickly. Up-spiral bits work well in cutting mortises or cavities when the cut does not pass all the way through the workpiece. Down spirals work best when the bit cuts all the way through the piece.

When talking about router bit performance, there's a tendency to consider just the bit. However, the bit is only part of the total picture. The kind of material you are working, the depth and width of the cut, the condition of the bit, and the speed that you move the router along the work (or feed the work past the bit) also make considerable differences.

One of the worst things you can do to a router bit is to try and cut too much in one pass. Make it a rule to complete multiple passes if you have to remove more than a ¼" square of material. Force feeding stresses the bit, makes it dull faster, and almost

Most router bits are created from bars of special hot-drawn steel on computer-controlled lathes. Each blank will go through eight to ten different steps on its way to becoming a finished bit.

always produces poor cuts.

Keep your bits clean with pitch and gum cleaner. Lubricate the bearing frequently. If you have the skill, you may want to hone the cutting edges of HSS bits after use to maintain a sharp cutting edge as long as possible. But don't even try to sharpen carbide bits—leave that task to a skilled professional sharpener.

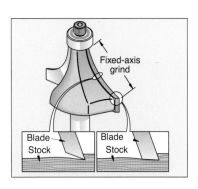

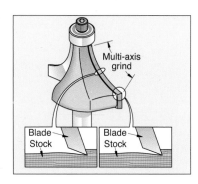

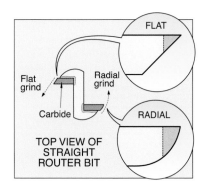

MAKING BITS LAST

SPECIAL FEATURE:

Here are some hints to help you get the most out of your router bit investment:

■ Never overload or abuse a bit. If the job calls for cutting away more than the equivalent of a ¼" square area, make multiple passes with light cuts only.

■ Consider a ⅜" square as the upside limit for most cuts.

■ For lots of heavy-duty routing, use ½" shank bits if your router accepts them. They're stronger, stiffer, easier to regrind, and they deflect less than other sizes.

■ Use bits with the shortest cutting-edge and the largest cutting diameter that you have on hand.

■ When possible, select bits with high hook angles and large gullets for fast chip ejection—they will run cooler and stay sharp longer.

■ Always use sharp bits. If you notice you're burning wood, having to apply extra force, or hearing chattering while cutting, you may have a dull bit.

■ If possible, use a router of 1½ hp or more—these cut at a faster feed rate and don't heat the bit as quickly as routers with less power.

■ When mounting a bit, insert the shank into the collet and finger-tighten the lock nut. Twist the bit several turns to let it seat itself. Then, lock the bit with ¾" to ⅞" of the shank captured in the collet. Do not insert the shank all the way to the bottom of the tool's collet.

■ Set router speed to spin the bit at its optimum rpm. Bits over 1" in diameter should be slowed to cut satisfactorily and not overheat.

■ Use a two-cutter system. Do most of the rough cutting with one bit, then make the final cut with a new or freshly ground bit with low "mileage."

■ Look for uneven cuts caused by extensive wear on a portion of the bit. This defect could produce poorly fitted joints. Sharpen or replace the offending bit.

■ Buy the highest quality bits you can afford.

■ Clean and lightly oil bits after each use.

■ Sand the shanks smooth with emery cloth. Clean and check the collet frequently for signs of wear.

■ Lubricate the ball bearings after each use.

■ Store your bits properly to avoid damage

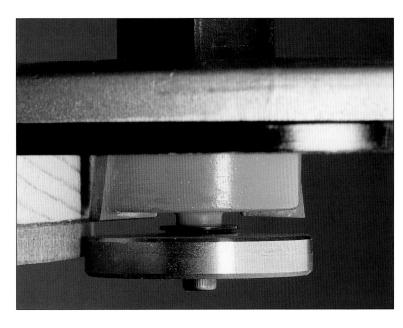

Mind the speed limits!

Although routers rely on high speed for good performance, larger bits should turn at slower speeds in order to keep the tip speed at a reasonable level. For example, a ¾"-diameter bit spinning at 22,000 rpm has a fairly mundane tip speed of 49 mph. By comparison, the tip speed on a 2½"-diameter bit spinning at the same rpm will hit 164 mph. Some experts suggest that a 130 to 140 mph tip speed should be the maximum for optimum performance and operator safety.

Bits you'll want to buy

On almost any furniture piece, you'll find examples of decorative treatments that you can reproduce with your own router. Demand created by the popularity of portable routers has resulted in a nearly limitless variety of bits being made available. The bits pictured on *pages 126* and *127* represent just some of the basic styles that woodworkers find useful.

Edge-forming bits cut decorative profiles along the edge

The bit tip affects plunge cutting. The extra cutting tooth in the center of the bit at left helps smooth the bottom and clear chips, although overall cut quality will be about the same for all three bits.

of the workpiece or cut one or both parts of an interlocking joint. Most have a pilot bearing on the end of the shank to ride along the edge of the workpiece to control cut width.

Field or surface-cutting bits have side and bottom cutting edges so they can cut into the surface of the workpiece and then be moved horizontally. They do not have a guide bearing so some type of guide—straightedge, edge

guide, or template guide bushing—must be used to keep the router moving straight or accurate. The cuts may be decorative or functional.

Speciality bits, as the name implies, encompass a large category of bits designed for

This bit has a dust shield and a relief grind under the bearing. With a relief grind, you can switch to a smaller bearing and use this cutting surface. Less expensive bits may not have any relief grind.

Suggested bit speeds for different diameter router bits:

Bit Diameter (inches)	Maximum Speed (rpm)
Up to 1"	up to 24,000
1 to 2½"	16,000 to 18,000
3"	12,000 to 14,500
3" or more	10,000 to 12,000

On core-box bits, look for a cleanly ground point on the bottom tip of the bit. Bits with steeper angles plunge easier, leaving a cleaner cut. On plunge cuts, bits must move chips fast to prevent burning.

unique routing tasks, either decorative or functional. The multi-profile bit, for example, has many different cutting edges. By changing its height in relation to the workpiece, you can cut an almost endless number of different profiles with it. A lock-miter bit, on the other hand, cuts a specific miter profile that's ideal for joining workpieces. (For more information about specialty bits, refer to Chapter 6.)

If you plan to work with plywood, you need to know about plywood bits. Plywood often is manufactured undersized or thinner than normal size. Put ½" plywood into a ½" dado and you'll get a poor fit. To help, some router bit manufacturers make undersized bits (⁷/₃₂", ²³/₃₂", 1¹/₃₂", and ¹⁵/₃₂").

Here's a suggested starter kit

With your first router you won't need specific bits right away, but consider buying these for starters (sizes refer to the diameter of the bit's bite): ¼", ⅜", and ½" straight bits; ¼", ⅜", and ½" round-overs; ³/₁₆", ⁵/₁₆", and ½" cove; ¼" radius and ⁵/₃₂" radius ogee; ¼" and ⅜" beading; and a ⅜" rabbeting bit with bearings.

To expand the list, you can add several spiral bits, a 45° chamfer bit, a 14°–½" dovetail bit, a ¼" round-nose bit, a ½" mortising bit, and a 90°–¼" V-grooving bit. This collection will enable you to make a wide variety of routing cuts.

Many companies offer sets of bits at substantial savings compared to what you'd pay if buying them individually. However, mentally subtract the bits you aren't likely to use, and then calculate the costs of those remaining to determine if the set is a good buy.

The lowdown on sharpening

Although people talk about sharpening router bits, wood-workers continually ask whether it really is practical (or even possible) to do so.

First, realize that router bits are an expendable item—they do wear and sometimes get damaged during use. Don't expect a bit to last forever. If it has given good service, but gone blunt, it may be best to simply replace it.

That said, several manufacturers we contacted agreed that the life of some carbide tipped bits might be extended if the flat surfaces are properly honed after use. However,

they caution, never attempt to hone the bevel. Bits must be perfectly balanced in order to spin at their high operating speed. The slightest difference in amount of material removed from one side of a bit than the other will create unbalance in the bit and cause dangerous vibration.

Honing carbide requires diamond wetstones. Three progressive grits—coarse 325 grit, fine 600 grit, and extra fine 1,200 grit—are typically used. They can be used dry, or lubricated with water, or a light oil such as WD-40. Just place the flat surface on the tip of the stone, and slide it along the stone. If the bit has two or more tips, make the same number of equal-length strokes and with the same light pressure to each face to avoid unbalancing the bit. Also, as you move to the finer grits, reduce pressure so as not to dislodge the diamonds from the bonding surface.

If you have a bit that you can't restore by lapping the face, consider sending it to a sharpening service. Wood-workers report valuable results from bits sharpened by commercial vendors, so there's no way to predict what kind of results you'll get. Considering the cost of the service and postage, it may be less expensive to replace the bit.

For HSS bits, lap the flat surfaces on fine-grit water-stones. Again, do the same amount of work to each surface to maintain proper balance and sharp edges.

A ROUTER BIT SAMPLER
EDGING router bits

ROUND-OVER
Uses: On tables, shelves, stair treads, and other projects. Making dowels, relieving sharp edges.
Sizes: Cutting radius ⅛–¾".

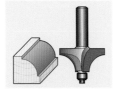

BEADING
Uses: Decorative edges on drawer fronts, cabinets, furniture, molding, and trim.
Sizes: Cutting radius ⅛–¾".

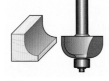

COVE
Uses: Decorative edges on drawer fronts, cabinets, furniture, molding, and trim. Used in combination with round-over bit to make drop-leaf table edges.
Sizes: Cutting radius ⅛–¾".

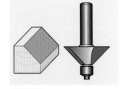

CHAMFER
Uses: Beveled edges on boards or laminates. Staved box and bowl construction.
Sizes: Cutting length ¼–1½", Bevels range from 7° to 45°.

RABBETING
Uses: Cutting rabbets and lap joints. Change bearing size to change rabbet width.
Sizes: Cutting width ⅛–½".

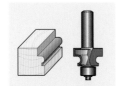

EDGE-BEADING
Uses: Forming decorative beads on edges of picture frames, moldings, and wainscoting.
Sizes: Bead diameter ⅛–¾".

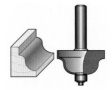

OGEE
Uses: Decorative edges on furniture, shelving, and molding.
Sizes: Cutting width 5⁄16–½".

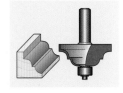

CLASSICAL
Uses: Decorative edges on furniture, shelving, and molding.
Sizes: Cutting width ⅜–½".

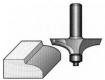

THUMBNAIL
Uses: Edge accent for tabletops, cabinet tops, chair rails, and hand rails.
Sizes: Cutting width 7⁄16–1".

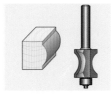

BULL-NOSE, HALF RADIUS
Uses: Curved profiles for stair treads, shelving, and windowsills.
Sizes: Cutting diameter ⅜–1½".

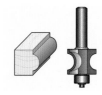

BULL-NOSE, FULL RADIUS
Uses: Half-round profiles for stair treads, shelving, finger grips, and windowsills. Making dowels.
Sizes: Cutting diameter 3⁄16–1½".

FLUTING
Uses: Round or square column accents. Classical molding. Combines with matching bull-nose, full-radius to make self-aligning joints for canoes, hot tubs, and planters.
Sizes: Cutting radius ⅛–3⁄16".

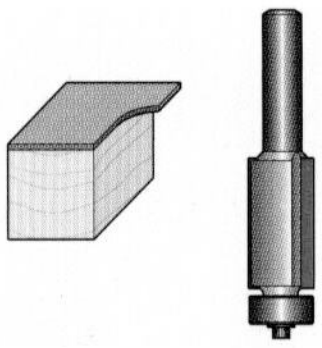

FLUSH-TRIM
Uses: Straighten and clean up edges of stock, flush-trim laminates, cutting around bottom-mounted templates, and edge molding.
Sizes: Cutting diameter ¼–¾".

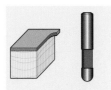

FLUSH-TRIM LAMINATE
Uses: Produce flush, square, and clean corners on plastic laminates, edge banding, and veneers.
Sizes: Cutting length ¼–⅜".

SPIRAL-FLUTE
Uses: Dadoing, grooving, and mortising. Up-spiral clears chips from hole. Down-spiral leaves a clean top edge on grooves and dadoes in veneers and plywood.
Sizes: Cutting diameter ⅛–¾".

FIELD router bits

STRAIGHT
Uses: Rabbeting, mortises, inlays, dadoes, box joints, spline joints.
Sizes: Cutting diameter 1/16–1¾".

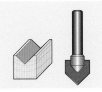

V-GROOVE
Uses: Lettering, veining, sign making, chamfering, decorative accents.
Sizes: Cutting diameter 1/8–1¾".

ROUND-NOSE CORE BOX
Uses: Fluting, veining, sign making, drawer-front finger pulls, decorative accents.
Sizes: Cutting diameter 1/8–2¼".

BOWL-AND-TRAY
Uses: Forming flat bottoms with rounded edges in trays and shallow bowls.
Sizes: Cutting diameter 7/16–1¼".

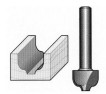

OGEE PLUNGE
Uses: Decorative grooves, and edge molding with a straightedge or router table.
Sizes: Cutting diameter 3/8–1⅛".

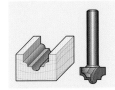

COVE-AND-BEAD PLUNGE
Uses: Decorative grooves, edge cutting with a straight-edge or router table.
Sizes: Cutting diameter ½–¾".

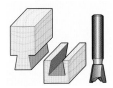

DOVETAIL
Uses: Decorative joints for drawers and boxes, sliding-drawer guides, sliding-dovetail joints for shelves, and chamfering.
Sizes: Cutting diameter ¼–1¼", cutter angles 7°–18°.

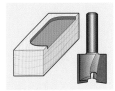

HINGE-MORTISE
Uses: Cutting smooth-bottom, shallow mortises for hinges and hardware when used with template guide bushing. Also functions as a straight bit and flush-trim bit.
Sizes: Cutting diameter 5/16–1½".

SPECIALTY router bits

RAISED PANEL
Uses: Cutting raised-panel profiles on cabinet- and passage-door panels. Use in a router table only. Requires special inserts in table to accept larger diameters.
Sizes: Cutting width 13/16–1½".

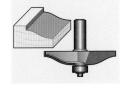

RAISED-PANEL OGEE
Uses: Cutting raised-panel profiles on cabinet- and passage-door panels. Use in a router table only. Requires special inserts in table to accept larger diameters.
Sizes: Cutting width 13/16–1½".

VERTICAL RAISED-PANEL
Uses: Cutting raised-panel profiles on cabinet- and passage-door panels. Use in a router table with fence. Can be used without special table inserts.
Sizes: Cutting width 1–1⅝".

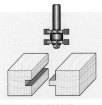

TONGUE-AND-GROOVE
Uses: Cutting tongue-and-groove joints for wall paneling, flooring, and panel doors. Making stub mortise-and-tenon joints. Vary beading size to adjust tongue depth.
Sizes: Most cut ¼" tongues and 3/8"-deep grooves.

ARCHITECTUAL MOLDING
Uses: Create wainscoting, chair rails, crown, and other architectural moldings. Dozens of profiles to choose from. Use with router table only.
Sizes: Cutting height 7/8–1¼".

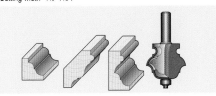

MULTI-FORM
Uses: Cuts dozens of different shapes using different parts of the bit profile and making multiple cutting passes at different depths. Can also use a spacer on the workpiece where the bearing rides for more shapes.
Sizes: Cutting height 1–1⅞".

SLOT CUTTER
Uses: Biscuit joinery, slots, lap joints, tongue and groove, and T-molding.
Sizes: Cutting height 1/16–¼".

6

Specialty Bits

*B*y now, you should realize that routers have an almost limitless capacity for woodworking projects. Well, that may be true, but it's the bits (and sets of bits) that perform the work. Here's an in-depth look at 14 types of bits designed for specific jobs, and some tips on how to use them.

ROUND-OVER BITS

Let's start with the most common of specialty bits. No other bit sees more action around the workshop than the round-over bit. Here's how to get the most from this routing workhorse.

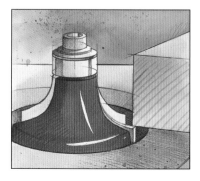

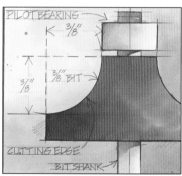

Match the bit to the project

Woodworking plans often specify that you round over an edge to a specific radius, say ½". Or, a plan may ask that you round over the edge with a certain bit, again say a ½" model. In either case, you'll need a bit that leaves an edge in the shape of a quarter-round with a ½" radius, as shown *top right*.

Manufacturers classify round-over bits according to the radius they cut. So, a ⅜" round-over bit cuts a ⅜" radius, and so forth. To determine the radius of a round-over bit,

measure either of its dimensions, as shown *middle right*.

The benefits of a rounded-over edge

Rounded edges give a project a softer, smoother look. The greater the radius of the round-over, the more pronounced this effect becomes.

Also, rounding an edge makes it more durable because it won't dent, splinter, or lose its finish as easily as a sharp corner. Like a knife that loses its sharp edge, a rounded corner is more "friendly" to people or other objects that come in contact with it.

A few keys to setting up a round-over bit

After mounting a round-over bit in a router, adjust the bit up or down so that the bottom of the concave cutting edge aligns flush with the router base or the surface of the router table. Use a flat block of wood, as shown *bottom right, opposite page,* to check your adjustment.

Before cutting your workpiece, test the cut on scrap stock. If the bit extends too far, it will cut a slight ridge into the workpiece surface. If the bit does not extend far enough, the radius will be incomplete.

How to cut a round-over with fillet

By extending the bit slightly, you can cut a round-over with fillet like the one *below.* Use a rule to precisely set the depth of the fillet as shown at *top.*

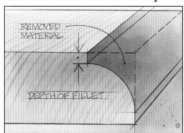

Convert a round-over bit into a beading bit

By simply changing to a smaller pilot bearing, you can make a round-over bit cut a beaded edge like the one *middle right.*

To change bearings, simply loosen the set screw atop the bearing with a hex wrench as shown at *bottom.* Buying a few bearings costs a lot less than dedicated beading bits!

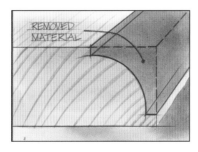

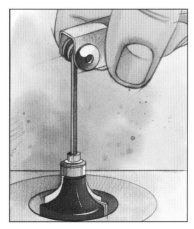

RAIL-AND-STILE BITS

Also called stile-and-rail, cope-and-stick, or cope-and-pattern bits, all rail-and-stile bits help you make frames, such as the one shown below left, from ¾"- to ⅞"-thick stock.

In one pass, these bits will cut interlocking joints for the frame pieces, impart a decorative profile, and leave a groove for holding the door panel. Frame-and-panels like this are traditionally used for cabinet doors, but also may be used for cabinet sides, furniture components, or for paneled walls and ceilings.

Note that the frame requires two cuts—a coped cut on the ends of the rails and a profiled cut on the inside edges of the rails and stiles. The profiled cut produces a groove for holding a panel. You can either make these cuts with a single bit that you lower and raise in your router table to make the two cuts, a single bit with cutters that you reconfigure, or separate bits. The choice is yours, but here's a look at the pros and cons of each.

One-piece bits

In this type, there are two styles. The type shown at *right* has a bearing in the center of the assembly, and two profile cutters in the same orientation.

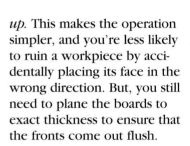

Another style has bearings above and below the cutting portion of the bit, as shown *below*. The profiled cutting edges are oriented opposite one another.

These bits fall in a mid-price range, costing approximately $70–$105, depending on the supplier. With these bits you do not have to reconfigure the cutters to change from a coped cut to a profiled cut. You simply raise the height of the bit in your router table.

With the one-bearing style of this bit, you make the coped cut with the *face side of the stock up* and the profiled cut with the *face side down,* just as you do with the one-piece reversible models. With the two-bearing bit you make both cuts with the workpieces *face side*

up. This makes the operation simpler, and you're less likely to ruin a workpiece by accidentally placing its face in the wrong direction. But, you still need to plane the boards to exact thickness to ensure that the fronts come out flush.

One-piece reversible bits

At $45–$65, these bits are your least costly option. They consist of a bearing, slotting cutter, and profile cutter stacked on a ¼" or ½" work arbor. ***Note: Due to the considerable mass of rail-and-stile bits, it's best to stick with models with ½" work arbors or shanks. Also, for the sake of safety and accuracy, use them only in a router table.***

One-piece reversible bits require considerable setup time because you need to switch the order of the bearing and cutters for

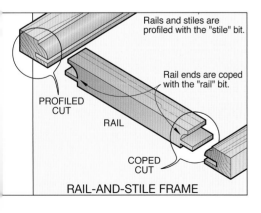

Rails and stiles are profiled with the "stile" bit.

Rail ends are coped with the "rail" bit.

PROFILED CUT

RAIL

COPED CUT

RAIL-AND-STILE FRAME

the coped and profiled cuts. This can be a little tricky, because you need to add thin metal washers (called shims) between the components to cut tight-fitting workpieces. Also, you need to remember to make the coped cuts with the rails *face side up,* and the profiled cuts with rails and stiles *face side down*.

Because you don't make both cuts with the face side down, it's essential that your stock be planed to exactly the same thickness—otherwise, the faces of the rails and stiles will not be flush with one another after assembly.

Two-piece adjustable bits

These bits cost $100–$125 per set, making them your most expensive option. Of course, they offer a number of advantages that justify their added cost.

With these sets you have separate bits for the coped and profiled cuts. For both cuts, you place all workpieces

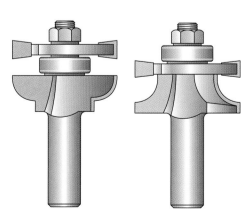

face side down. Because the faces are referenced off the router tabletop, they always come out flush on the face side (provided the bits are adjusted properly), even if your workpieces vary slightly in thickness.

With these bits you also have a greater selection of styles than the one-piece sets. In addition to ogee, straight bevel, and cove-and-bead styles, which are available with all types of rail-and-stile bits, manufacturers of two-piece sets offer you bead and round-over profiles, such as the ones shown *below left*.

Two-piece non-adjustable bits

These mid-priced bits (about $75 per set) work like the two-piece adjustable versions insofar as you position the face sides of your workpieces down for both cuts. These bits, *above right,* usually make acceptable cuts, but the joints can be slightly looser than those you'll cut with the other types of bits. And, the joints will become looser each time you sharpen the bits because you can't adjust the spacing between their cutting edges.

In testing, it was found that the bearings located at the top of the bits were too high to contact a ¾"-thick workpiece. And, these bearings do not provide an accurate reference for aligning your router-table fence (read on to find out how to do this).

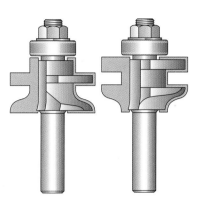

Which type is best for you?

Regardless of your budget, your best choice is either the one-piece bit or one of the two-piece adjustable sets.

If you want to keep things as simple as possible, go for the one-piece bit. You'll get tight joints with no shimming. You do need to plane your work-pieces to exact thickness, but that's a good rule to follow regardless of which bit you use.

Because you cannot adjust the cutters in this bit, your joints will become slightly looser with each sharpening. However, this bit will help you make many door frames before it produces unaccept-able joints. A home wood-worker may never make enough door frames to require sharpening the bit.

For $10–$35 more, a two-piece adjustable set gives you a greater selection of styles (including the popular round-over), and can be adjusted after sharpenings. It also sits lower during the profiled cut, which seems safer than the tall one-piece bits.

SPECIAL FEATURE: GETTING THE BEST RESULTS FROM RAIL-AND-STILE BITS

Like most everything, the key to success with rail-and-stile bits is in the setup. You need to set up the bits for coped and profiled cuts that fit tightly together, and self-align the faces flush with each other. Although the various types of rail-and-stile bits require slightly different bit adjustments and workpiece orientation, the basic procedure is similar for all of them. Here's how to get great results with a two-piece adjustable set.

Note: It's always a good idea to test your router-table setups with scrap stock. Also, use scrap stock for Steps 2, 3, and 4 after each bit resharpening. Once you are satisfied that the bits will produce tight-fitting joints (you may need to add metal shims to those bits that accept them), cut your rails and stiles to length. If you've never used these bits before, it's a good idea to make several complete frames using scrap stock.

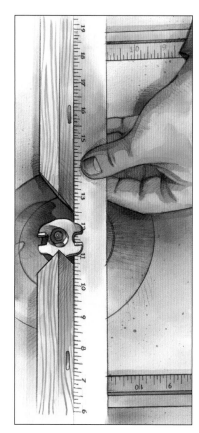

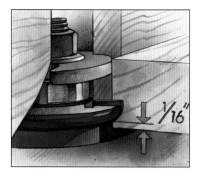

1 Set up the fence

With a straightedge at least as long as your router-table fence and a pair of 12" rules, align the fence flush with the bearing on the "rail" bit (the bit with the bearing in its middle), and parallel with the miter-gauge slot. If your router table doesn't have a miter-gauge slot, just align the fence and bearing flush.

2 Elevate the rail bit for the coped cuts

Using a scrap of wood as an aid, adjust the rail bit so there's a space of about ¹⁄₁₆"

between the table and the profile portion of the rail bit, as shown *above*.

3 Cut the end grain on the rails

First, attach a ¾" plywood auxiliary face to your miter-gauge. The auxiliary face should butt against the router-table fence. (This piece supports the workpiece and helps prevent grain tearout on the exit side of the cut.) Then, hold the rail face down, with either edge firmly against the miter gauge, and its end butted against the fence. Turn on the router and slowly rout the workpiece to make the coped cut. Turn the

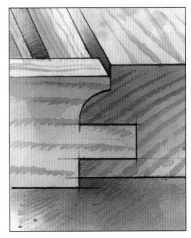

rail around, keeping its face side down, and cut its other end. Repeat this procedure for all of your rails.

If your router table doesn't have a miter-gauge slot, you can use a ¾ × 10 × 12" scrap of plywood against the fence, and hold the rail against the adjacent edge facing the router bit.

4 Set the stile bit for end-grain profiled cuts

Install the stile bit and elevate it so its slot cutter aligns with the tenon on a rail end, as

shown *below.* Make an edge-grain cut in a piece of scrap stock of the same thickness as your rails and stiles.

5 Check your results and make needed adjustments

Fit together the scrap piece you just cut and one of your rail ends. Both faces should align flush. If they don't, you'll need to adjust the height of the stile bit. In the example *top right,* the stile bit needs to be adjusted down.

6 Make the edge-grain cuts

Pass the inside edges of the rails and stiles through the stile bit, face down. That's it—you should have the components for a perfect rail-and-stile frame!

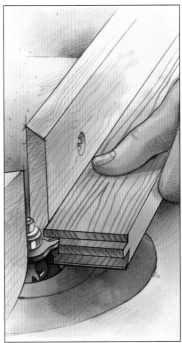

VERTICAL RAISED-PANEL BITS

These bits are increasingly popular because they don't require the use of a big, variable-speed router. But, there are some tradeoffs you need to consider.

Pros and cons

Because vertical bits don't exceed 1½" in diameter, you can run them at full speed (about 24,000 rpm). So, most single-speed routers with at least 1½ hp will handle them.

You can buy these bits for $45 to $60 each—in the same ballpark as horizontal bits. Vertical bits have ½" shanks, and cut the same profiles (ogee, cove, or straight bevel) and the same reveal (about 1½") as full-size horizontal bits.

As you will see, vertical bits will cut almost as smoothly as horizontal bits, but only if you take your time and work slowly. You shouldn't find their slow pace a problem if you plan on making just a few panels.

Finally, vertical bits can only make cuts along straight edges. So, they won't help you if you're making arch-topped panels.

How to get smooth results

Important tip: Build the frame that the panel will fit into before you start the following procedures. Then, you can test-fit your first panel and be confident that all of your panels will fit into their frame grooves. These bits are designed to be used with ¾"-thick stock.

With vertical panel-raising bits, workpieces are stood on edge as they are fed, so you'll need a tall router-table fence for support. You'll most likely have success with the fence shown *opposite top*. It has a guide bar that holds the bottom of the panel in firm contact with the router bit for a consistent cut. It also helps to keep your hands away from the bit.

After building the fence, clamp the guide bar in place, adjusting it so a panel snugly fits between the bar and fence. The panel should slide smoothly, but without any

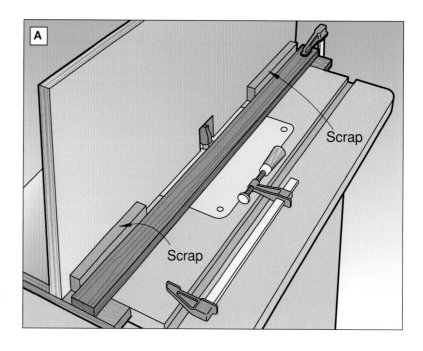

A

Scrap

Scrap

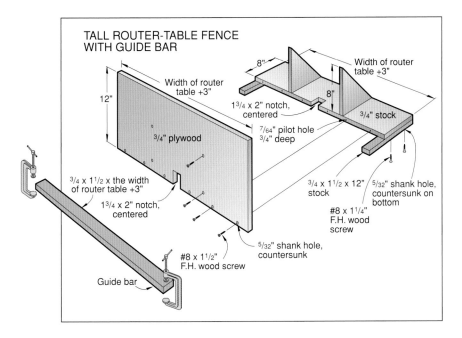

TALL ROUTER-TABLE FENCE
WITH GUIDE BAR

12"

Width of router
table +3"

8"

$1^{3}/_{4}$ x 2" notch,
centered

Width of router
table +3"

8"

$3/_4$" stock

$3/_4$" plywood

$7/_{64}$" pilot hole
$3/_4$" deep

$3/_4$ x $1^{1}/_2$ x the width
of router table +3"

$1^{3}/_{4}$ x 2" notch,
centered

$3/_4$ x $1^{1}/_2$ x 12"
stock

$5/_{32}$" shank hole,
countersunk on
bottom

#8 x $1^{1}/_4$"
F.H. wood
screw

#8 x $1^{1}/_2$"
F.H. wood screw

$5/_{32}$" shank hole,
countersunk

Guide bar

B

Feed
direction
0

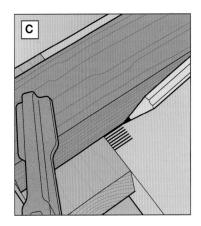

C

$1/_{16}$" of its carbide cutting edge is above the table surface. Clamp the fence to the router table so the bit makes a cut about $1/_{16}$" deep.

Hold your panel as shown in Illustration B, and make a cut along the end grain. Hold the top of the panel in solid contact with the fence, being careful not to tip the bottom of the panel into the bit. Feed the workpiece slowly to prevent scalloped cuts and grain tearout. (The ends are especially susceptible to tearout.) Try not to pause as you feed, or the bits will burn the wood. Make the same cut along the opposite end, and then cut the edge-grain sides.

With a pencil, mark the position of the fence on both ends of the table, as shown in Illustration C. These marks will help you reposition the fence for subsequent panels. Then, readjust the fence for another $1/_{16}$"-deep cut. Make the cuts, remembering to cut the ends first, and again mark the position of the fence. Repeat this procedure until you cut the profile to its final depth.

slop. We positioned the bar by placing two pieces of scrap panel stock between the fence and bar, as shown in Illustration A on the *opposite page*.

Now, install the bit and adjust its height so that all but

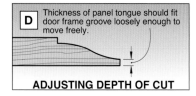

D Thickness of panel tongue should fit door frame groove loosely enough to move freely.

ADJUSTING DEPTH OF CUT

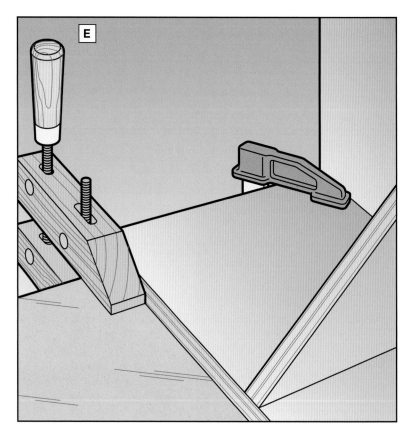

Depending on the wood, you may be able to take deeper cuts without any problem. But, it's best to err on the side of shallow cuts—even when you get smooth results with deeper cuts. Why? Large chunks of wood can unexpectedly break free from hard, open-grained woods, such as red oak, seriously marring the panel.

As you approach the final depth (the panel edges should be about ¼" thick), check the panel for fit into the frame groove according to the guideline in Illustration D. If you're making multiple panels, clamp some stops onto the table at back of the fence as shown in Illustration E—these will guarantee cuts of uniform depth on all of your pieces.

The final verdict

If you already own a 3-hp, variable-speed router, or can

afford to buy one, go with horizontal bits for panel raising. They don't require any special jigs, but you may need an auxiliary tabletop if your router-table plate doesn't have insert rings for bits of various diameters. And, you'll get better results in much less time.

Vertical raised-panel bits make sense if you need to make a few panels and don't want to spend more than $200 on a large router. Just remember to take your time!

FINGER-JOINT BITS

These bits will help you make super-strong end-to-end joints, but proper setup can be tricky. The following method should help you succeed time after time.

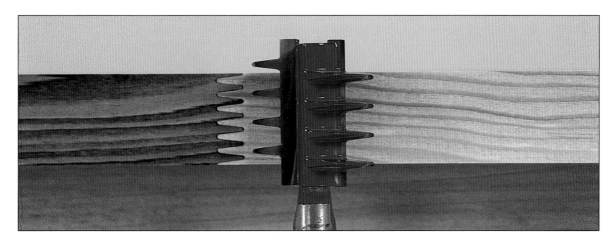

Advantages and uses

It's usually simple to glue edge or face surfaces together, but gluing boards end-to-end is another matter entirely. This is because the hollow fibers of the end-grain work like straws to draw adhesive away from a joint. Plus, the ends of these "straws" provide very little surface area for the glue to adhere to.

Fortunately, a finger-joint bit will help solve both of these problems by exposing face grain and greatly increasing the surface area of the joint.

With one of these bits, you can make good use of your scrap stock by end-joining short pieces to make longer ones. But, because the edge-grain view of a finger joint can be less than appealing, use it only for outdoor projects or pieces that will be painted.

Seven steps to great results

There are several types of finger-joint bits available, including ones with variable-spaced cutters and bearings. These instructions refer particularly to a very basic version, such as the one shown *above*—a one-piece cutter without a bearing. With this eight-finger bit, you can finger-joint stock up to 1 $\frac{1}{16}$" thick in one pass.

1 Set the bit upright and rotate it so the highest finger faces you. With a permanent pen, mark the third finger down on the side facing you, as shown in the drawing *above right*. This will be the reference finger for the steps to follow.

2 Mark a centerline along the edge of a scrap piece that's the same thickness as your workpiece. With the bit in your router table, adjust the height so the point of the reference finger aligns with the centerline as shown *at bottom*.

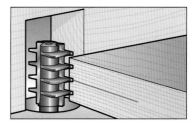

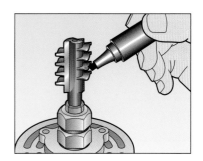

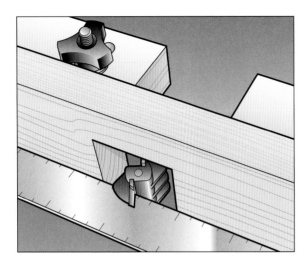

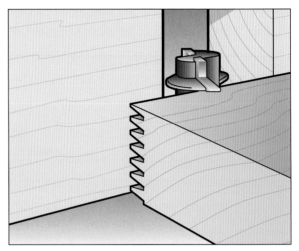

3 With the router unplugged, rotate the bit by hand to the point where it makes the deepest possible cut into the workpiece. Then, use a straight-edge to align the fence flush with the innermost cutting edge of the fingers (the "web" of the fingers, so to speak). Also, the fence should be parallel to your router table's miter-gauge slot.

4 Test the fence position by making a test cut into the edge grain of your scrap stock. If the fingers that you just cut into the workpiece do not contact the exit side of the fence (*above right*), you need to decrease the depth of the cut by bringing the fence forward. If the workpiece fingers contact the fence, but are not smooth and rounded on their ends, you need to increase the cutting depth. In order to do this, adjust the fence back.

5 Cut the edges of two pieces of scrap stock, flip one piece over, and place the finger-jointed edges together. The faces should align flush. If they don't, you'll need to adjust the bit's height up or down by half of the misalignment between the faces of the scrap stock.

In the example shown *below,* the faces are misaligned by about 1/16". So, we *lowered* the bit 1/32". Conversely, if the piece on the right side of the illustration were 1/16" too high, we would *raise* the bit by 1/32".

6 Now you're ready to cut your actual workpieces! First, attach an auxiliary fence to your miter gauge. The end of the fence should contact the router-table fence without preventing you from pushing the miter gauge smoothly through its complete travel. Place one edge of a work-

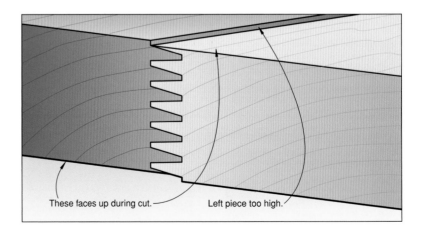

These faces up during cut. —   Left piece too high.

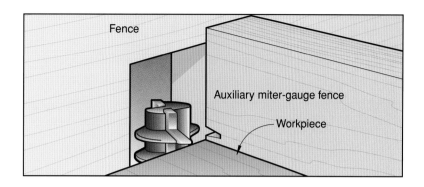

piece against the auxiliary fence, butt the end of the workpiece against the router-table fence, and make a cut by pushing the miter gauge forward—*slowly but steadily*. (The face side of the workpiece can be either up or down.) The auxiliary fence backs up the work-piece to prevent edge-grain chipping on the exit end of the cut.

To cut the other end, flip the workpiece *end-over-end* and repeat the procedure described above. DO NOT simply rotate the piece and keep its same face down for the second cut. By flipping the workpiece, you will ensure that the face sides of your workpieces will be on the same side of your com-pleted assembly.

7 Apply glue to the finger-jointed ends by running a thin bead of wood-worker's glue between each finger. Work the glue into the fingers, as shown here, so it covers all surfaces. (It doesn't pay to apply glue to both sur-faces of a finger-joint. This will just create excessive glue squeeze-out).

After applying the glue, join the two workpieces and rub them back and forth to ensure that all surfaces of the joint receive glue.

RULE-JOINT BITS

Drop-leaf tables have always had a certain popularity because of their "now you see them, now you don't" nature. With the drop-leaves up, you gain tabletop. With them down, you add floor space. The joint that does the work is called a rule joint.

To make the rule joint between the tabletop and drop-leaf, you cut the edges of the tabletop with a round-over bit, then use a cove bit of the same radius to cut the mating edge on the leaf. These bits are typically sold in matching "rule bit" or "drop-leaf table" sets like the one shown *above right*. Here, a ½"-radius set for ¾"-thick stock was used.

To complete the job, you'll also need a router table and two drop-leaf hinges for each leaf. These special hinges have one leaf that is longer than the other. Let's get started.

1 Install the round-over bit in your table-mounted router, and adjust the table's fence so the bit's bearing extends just barely beyond the fence (check this with a straightedge). Set the height of the bit so it makes a beading cut with a ⅛" shoulder, as shown at *right, top* . Rout all four edges of the tabletop, profiling the end-grain edges first. (If the table will be placed against a wall, you may elect not to rout the edge facing the wall.) Also, rout all of the edges of the drop-leaf, except for the edge that mates with the tabletop.

2 Install the cove bit with its bearing extending just beyond the fence. With a piece of scrap of the same thickness as your workpiece, make a cut that leaves a ⁷⁄₆₄" shoulder, as shown *bottom*. Adjust the height of the bit until the scrap piece and the

tabletop have a uniform ¹⁄₆₄" gap between them, as shown *opposite*. You can check this gap by using a playing card as a type of feeler gauge. Rout the drop-leaf edge that mates with the tabletop.

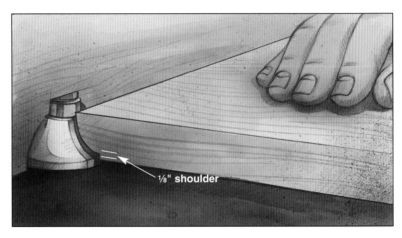

⅛" shoulder

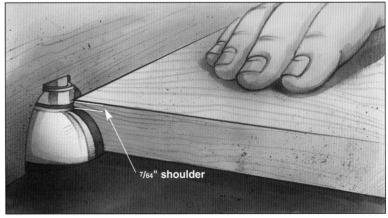

⁷⁄₆₄" shoulder

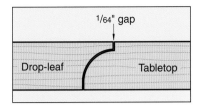

1/64" gap

Drop-leaf   Tabletop

3 With the bottom side of the table facing up, mark the position of the hinges by first drawing a line set back and parallel to the edge that mates with the drop-leaf, as shown *below*. This setback should equal the radius of your rule-joint bits. Now, mark the position of the two hinges on this line, as shown here.

4 With a straight bit, rout a pair of mortises in the locations determined in the previous step, as shown *below, top right*. Be sure to rout the mortises deep and wide enough to accommodate the hinge's pivot. Clamp a straightedge to the table to guide the cut.

5 Align the tabletop and mating leaf, both bottom side up. To maintain the 1/64" gap between them, place playing cards as shown, just to the depth of

their shoulders. Drill pilot holes and attach the hinges. (If you elect to mortise the hinge leafs, mark their locations, then rout and chisel out the waste area before screwing down the hinges.)

6 Add a means for supporting the drop leaf. You can either buy metal brackets, add a piece of wood that slides out from beneath the tabletop, or build a gatelike leg that swings out from the base of the table.

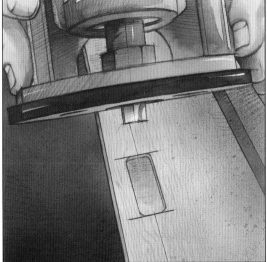

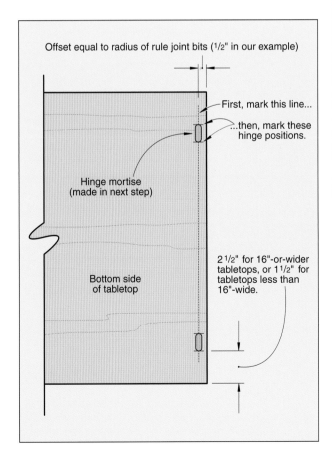

Offset equal to radius of rule joint bits (1/2" in our example)

First, mark this line...

...then, mark these hinge positions.

Hinge mortise (made in next step)

Bottom side of tabletop

2 1/2" for 16"-or-wider tabletops, or 1 1/2" for tabletops less than 16"-wide.

WINDOW-SASH SET

If you've always shied away from building your own custom windows or French doors because you thought the task was too involved, you'll appreciate this bit set. It will help you achieve great results without a lot of fuss.

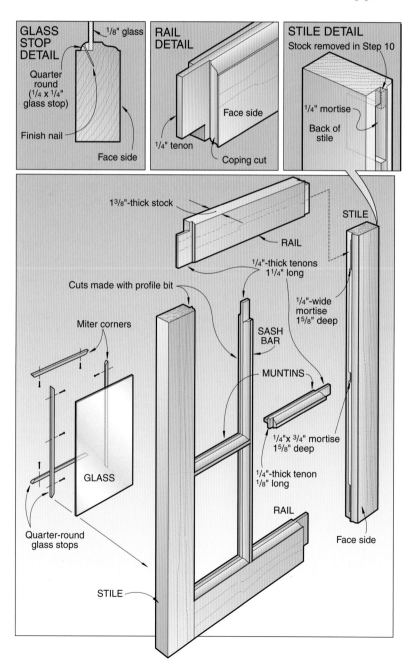

GLASS STOP DETAIL

1/8" glass

Quarter round (1/4 x 1/4" glass stop)

Finish nail

Face side

RAIL DETAIL

Face side

1/4" tenon

Coping cut

STILE DETAIL

Stock removed in Step 10

1/4" mortise

Back of stile

1³⁄₈"-thick stock

RAIL

STILE

1/4"-thick tenons 1¹⁄₄" long

1/4"-wide mortise 1⁵⁄₈" deep

SASH BAR

Cuts made with profile bit

MUNTINS

Miter corners

1/4"x 3/4" mortise 1⁵⁄₈" deep

GLASS

1/4"-thick tenon 1/8" long

RAIL

Quarter-round glass stops

Face side

STILE

Window sash sets consist of two bits like those shown here. With these you can make traditionally styled rail-and-stile frames with coped joints and a rabbeted side for accepting glass. You also can make the narrow sash bars and muntins for holding multiple panes of glass. All of the coped joints are reinforced with tenons for long-lasting durability.

Because you will be plowing these bits through 1³⁄₈"-thick stock, they come with sturdy ½" shanks. For safety and good results, use them with a router rated at 1½ hp or more, mounted in a table.

1 Cut your stiles, rails, sash bars, and muntins to width and length from 1³⁄₈"-thick stock. Here's how to calculate the lengths of your parts (using an 18 × 24" window with 3"-wide rails and stiles as an example):

First, cut the stiles to the full height of the window (24"). To figure rail length, subtract the combined width of the stiles (6") from the finished width of the window (18"). To this number (12"), add the length of two tenons (1¼" + 1¼") and ½" (for the coped joint). So, for our example, the rails were cut 15" long. Cut the sash bars and muntins ¾" wide and calculate their lengths as you did the rails. (Plan to cut 1¼"-long tenons on both ends of the sash bar and muntins; you'll trim the muntin tenons that intersect with the sash bars to ⅛" long later.)

2 Mark the face side of your workpieces (the inside surface of your window or the most-viewed side of your door). Also, mark the outside edges of the rails and stiles, and place marks centered on the rails and stiles where they intersect with the muntins and sash bar, and on the sash bar where it intersects with the muntins.

3 To cut 1¼" tenons on both ends of the rails, sash bars, and muntins, install a full-width dado set in your tablesaw and adjust it for a ⅝"-high cut. Position the saw's fence 1¼" from the side of the dado set farthest from the fence. Place the workpiece on the tablesaw face down with one edge against a miter gauge, and one end against the fence. Make the cut in multiple passes, as shown in Illustrations A and B.

4 Position the rail, sash bar, or muntin face side up on the tablesaw. Place a

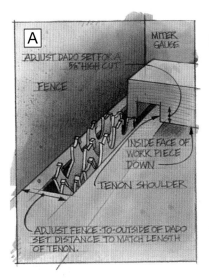

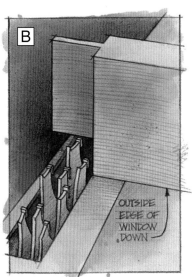

⅛" spacer between the workpiece and tablesaw top, as shown in Illustration C, and make the same cut as described in the previous step. Your tenons should be ¼" thick.

5 Complete the tenon cuts on the rails by placing them outside edge down on the tablesaw. Make multiple cuts with the dado set ⅝" high as before.

6 Install the coping bit in your router table. Place the face side of a rail on the table and adjust the coping bit up so the tops of its cutters contact the tenon (Illustration D). With the fence adjusted so the coping bit cuts ¼" past the tenon shoulder, cut both ends of the rails, sash bar, and muntins. (For a 1¼"-long tenon, set the fence 1½" from the cutter tip with the tip rotated to its farthest distance from the fence.)

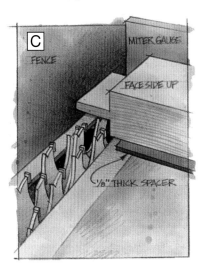

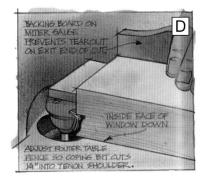

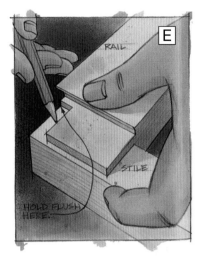

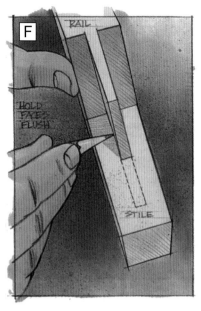

mortises that hold the sash bar and muntin tenons. Cut the mortises ⅜" deeper than the length of the tenons. The mortise in the sash bar will go completely through it.

8 Install the profile bit in your router table and adjust it as shown in Illustration G. With the face side of the workpiece down, mold the inside edges of the rails and stiles.

9 To perform the same operation on the sash bar and muntins, clamp a secondary fence onto the router table as shown in in Illustration H. Make this fence from 1¼"-thick stock, and position it so the sash bar and muntins slide snugly between it and the main router table fence.

7 Mark the positions of the mortises on the stiles by using the tenon that mates with it. First, as shown in Illustration E, stand the stile inside edge up on a work surface and position the rail to mark the length of the mortise.

Then, rest the rail on top of the stile, as shown in Illustration F, to mark the mortise width. Use the same steps to mark the position of the

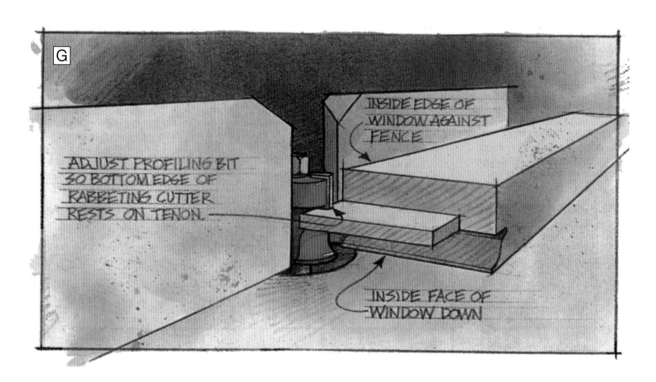

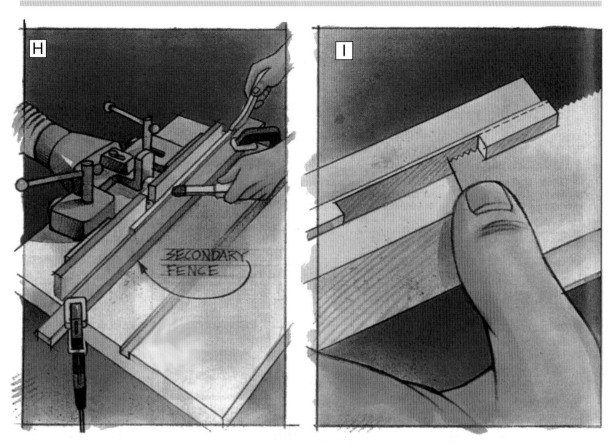

10 Mold both edges of the sash bar and muntins. Use pushsticks to pass the stock between the fences.

Use a fine-toothed saw to remove the small amount of material on the outside end of each stile mortise, as shown in Illustration I and in the Stile Detail drawing on *page 144*. If you're making more than one window or door, you may want to set up a router table with a straight bit to do this more quickly.

Now is a good time to trim the muntin tenons that intersect the sash bar. Cut them to ⅛" long.

11 Assemble the project without glue to check for fit and squareness. Disassemble, apply glue to all mating surfaces, and apply clamps. Check for square again before the glue sets.

12 Install the glass in the rabbeted openings on the back face of the door or window. Each pane should be ⅛" smaller in width and length than the rabbeted opening it fits into. Mount the glass in place with glazing points and glazing putty, or with quarter-round strips of wood mitered on their ends and nailed down. (See the Glass Stop Detail drawing on *page 144*).

CHAMFER BITS

Although better known in the workshop for easing (softening) exposed edges, chamfer bits also can cut dead-on miters for end-to-end or edge-to-edge joining.

5 CHAMFER BITS AND THE MITERS THEY CUT					
ROUTER BIT					
CUTTER ANGLE	11.25°	15°	22.5°	30°	45°
NUMBER OF SIDES IN BOX	16	12	8	6	4
END-TO-END JOINED WORKPIECES					
EDGE-TO-EDGE JOINED WORKPIECES					

As you can see in the chart, chamfer bits come in five cutter angles for making boxes with various numbers of sides. Note that the 45-degree bit shown is considerably larger than the others—that's because it's capable of making a full-edge cut in ¾"-thick stock (a nice advantage). For all ¾" material, you'll need the largest 45-

degree bit available—one with a cutting diameter of 2½" or more.

Note also in the chart that there are two kinds of miter cuts you can make with chamfer bits: end-grain miters (for shallow boxes or frames), and edge-grain miters (for deeper boxes). Here, you'll find out how to make both types using a table-mounted router.

How to miter end-to-end joined workpieces

First, install the chamfer bit and adjust its height so the bottoms of its cutting edges are just below table level. Then, set your router table's miter gauge precisely 90° to its miter slot. Add a wood auxiliary face to the miter gauge

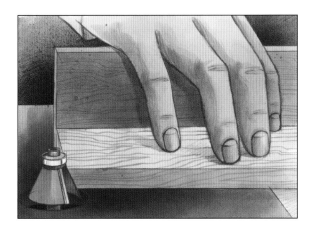

that extends up to, but just a hair shy of, the chamfer bit's pilot bearing.

Note: Perform each of the following steps on all of your workpieces before moving on to the next step.

1 Rip your stock to exact width and crosscut your workpieces about ⅛" too long. Miter one end, as shown *above left.* For best control make multiple shallow cuts until the bit miters the entire workpiece end.

2 Cut a full miter on the opposite end, leaving each workpiece about ¹⁄₁₆" too long. Now, miter one workpiece to its final length. Then, use this workpiece to set a stopblock on the miter-gauge auxiliary fence. Cut all of the pieces, as shown *above right.*

Cutting miters for edge-to-edge project pieces

1 Rip and crosscut all of your workpieces to their finished width and length. Adjust the chamfer bit for a full-height cut and position your router table's fence for a shallow cut. Make this cut on both edges of all of the workpieces. Move the fence back for a slightly deeper cut

and repeat, doing this until your miter cuts on both edges come to within about ⅛" of the top of each workpiece.

2 Adjust the fence so the chamfer bit cuts the full miter without reducing the workpiece's width. (For precise results, make test cuts in scrap stock first.) Make your final miter cuts on both edges, as shown *below.*

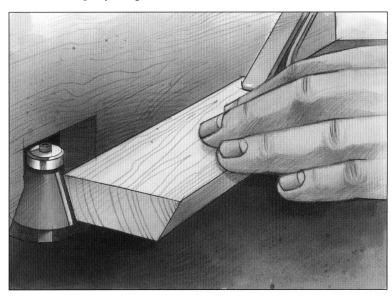

THE MULTI-PROFILE BIT—
A REAL HEAVYWEIGHT

With cutting wings about 2" in height and diameter, the multi-profile bit is among the largest router bits you can buy. Also known as a multi-form bit, this considerable mass of steel and carbide doesn't come cheap. You can expect to pay upward of $60 for high-quality versions of this bit.

Because of its hefty size, only use this bit mounted in a router table. And for safe and effective machining, your router should have a motor of at least 2 hp, a collet that accepts ½" shanks, and variable-speed control so you can slow it down to about 15,000 rpm. Also, be sure your router table and fence have bit openings of at least 2¼".

Too much bit for you?

If you don't own much of the equipment mentioned so far in this chapter, but you do have a full array of round-over, ogee, and cove bits, you may not need or want this behemoth bit. But, if you have a limited number of bit profiles, or just like to design your own custom ones, this bit may fill the bill. By varying the height of the bit and the orientation of your workpiece and making multiple passes, you can produce an unlimited array of profiles. A few possibilities are shown *below.*

Points to keep in mind

Because the pilot bearing doesn't come into play with most of the cuts you make with this bit, you will typically need to guide your workpieces against a fence. For that reason, you can't rout curved edges when cutting most profiles.

When cutting with the lower portion of the bit—below its widest point—you'll need to take several safety precautions. First and foremost, keep in your mind that a large portion of the bit is exposed above the workpiece surface. Keep your hands well clear of the bit, use a fence-mounted guard that shields the bit, and employ pushsticks as often as possible.

The portion of the bit above and overhanging the workpiece also can create potential kickback. If the workpiece should lift up during routing, it could strike the spinning bit and go flying. To prevent this calamity, hold the workpiece down firmly with feather boards mounted to the fence on both the infeed and outfeed sides of the bit.

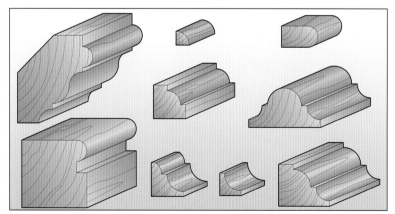
Some of the profiles you can cut with a multi-profile bit.

DRAWER-LOCK BITS

The unique geometry of the drawer-lock bit creates a strong bond between perpendicular pieces. The joints you'll produce will not only be strong, but attractive as well.

The wedge-shaped tenons formed by a drawer-lock bit self-align both workpieces for a perfectly mating joint. Moreover, once you've set the bit to the correct height, you need only adjust your router-table fence to make a variety of mating cuts. Remember this, though: For safety, a drawer-lock bit should always be used in a router table, *never* in a handheld router.

Setting up your router table and milling the fronts

1 If your router table doesn't have a split fence, you'll need to build out the fence almost the full diameter of the bit. That's because most of the bit must be captured inside the fence when milling drawer or box sides.

Close the opening around the bit by making an auxiliary

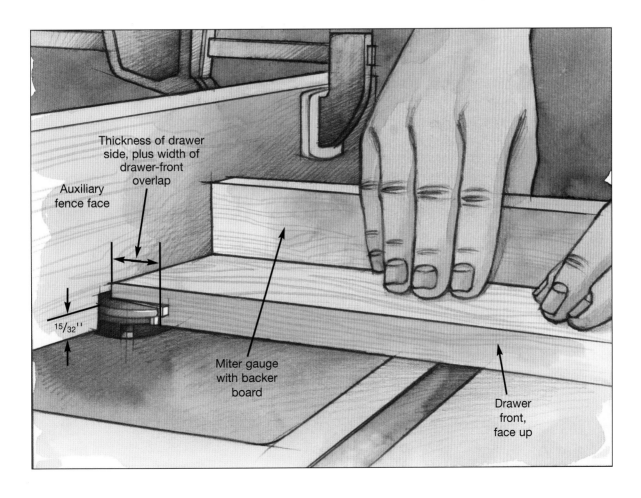

Thickness of drawer side, plus width of drawer-front overlap

Auxiliary fence face

15/32"

Miter gauge with backer board

Drawer front, face up

face for your router-table fence. For our 2"- diameter bit, we cut a ⅝ x 2¼" dado in a scrap of ½" medium-density fiberboard (MDF), then clamped it to the router-table fence with the dado centered over the bit, as shown on *page 151*.

2 Mount the drawer-lock bit in your table-mounted router, and set the top of the cutter so that it's ¹⁵⁄₃₂" above the tabletop.

3 Calculate the fence position by adding your drawer front's intended overlap (if any) and the thick-

ness of your drawer side. Position your router-table fence that same distance back from the upper cutting edge of the bit.

For example, if your drawer front will overlap the sides by ⅜", and the sides are ½"-thick, put the fence ⅞" back from the upper part of the bit. For flush-mount drawers, or drawers to which you'll add a false front, place the fence only the thickness of the drawer side from the bit's upper cutting edge.

You also could use this dimension for milling the drawer backs. But cutting the backs with the same overlap

as the fronts, then trimming them to size, ensures that the inside dimensions of the drawer will remain constant.

4 To prevent tearout while milling the fronts, attach a backer board to your miter gauge so that the backer board just touches the auxiliary fence face, as shown on *page 151*.

5 With your drawer front cut to finished size, place it faceup on the router table. Keep one end of the drawer front against the router-table fence and mill the

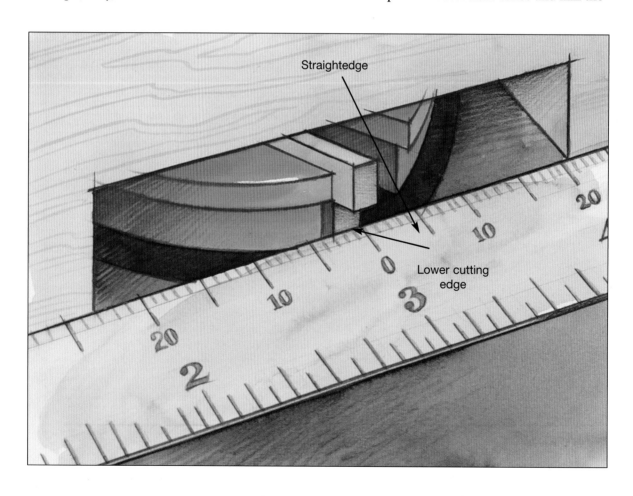

Straightedge

Lower cutting edge

workpiece using the miter gauge as a guide. Turn the workpiece around, keeping it face-up, and mill the other end. If you're making more than one drawer, machine all of the drawer fronts (and backs, if you like) using this router setup.

Now the drawer sides

1 Without changing the cutting height of the bit, move the fence so that it's flush with the lower cutting surface of the drawer-lock bit. You might try rotating the bit so the cutting edge is forward, then laying a straightedge against it for reference, as shown *opposite*.

2 To prevent tear-out, make a pushblock from scrap and an extra piece of drawer-side stock (or scrap of the same thickness), as shown *top right*. Make certain that the two pieces form a 90° angle, and that the screws are high enough to clear the cutting path of the bit.

3 Cut the drawer sides to size. Stand the drawer side on end, placing the inside face against the fence. Use the pushblock, as shown at *right*, to guide the drawer side through the bit.

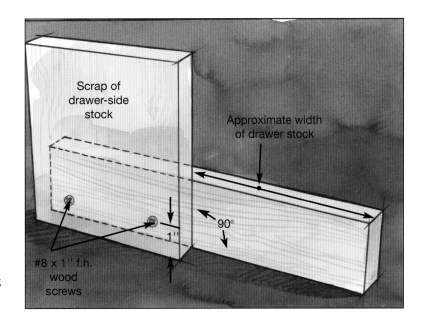

Scrap of drawer-side stock

Approximate width of drawer stock

90°

1"

#8 x 1" f.h. wood screws

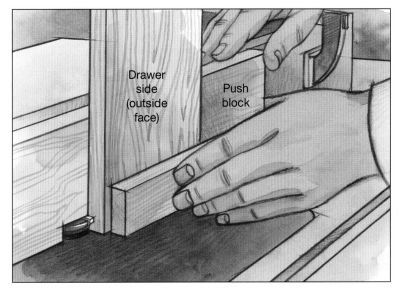

Drawer side (outside face)

Push block

SPIRAL BITS

While they might resemble a high-tech version of the classic barbershop pole, spiral bits do more than take a little off the top. You can use them wherever you'd use a straight bit, but you'll get cleaner cuts.

Spiral-fluted router bits leave the edges of your cuts virtually fray-free, because as they turn, the two corkscrew-shaped cutting edges stay in contact with your workpiece longer than the vertical cutting edges of a straight bit. This results in a shearing action instead of the rapid chop-chop-chop-chop of the traditional double-fluted straight bit.

Unlike most router bits that have a carbide cutter brazed to a steel bit body, spiral bits are made of solid carbide. Carbide is harder than steel, but also more brittle, so you must work with more care than with non-carbide bits. Don't force the work, and avoid sudden plunges or starts.

The following are the three kinds of spiral bits on the market—check them out to see which might be best for your task at hand.

Downcut

As the name implies, the cutting action of this bit is downward, or away from the router base. That shearing motion imparts a clean edge on rabbets, dadoes, grooves, shallow mortises, and plunge cuts in both sheet goods and solid stock.

When cutting grooves or dadoes deeper than the diameter of the bit, don't try to take the full depth at once. Instead, make several, progressively deeper, passes. A downcut bit tends to pack the wasted material down into a deep cut, rather than ejecting it, and shallow cuts reduce the problem.

Upcut

This bit wasn't designed to leave a clean edge like a downcut bit, but rather to remove the chips created in a deep plunge cut. That makes it ideal for plowing out a deep mortise in solid stock. Tear-out caused by the upward shearing will be hidden by the tenoned workpiece.

You also can use an upcut bit in your router table for any edge treatment that you perform with the workpiece

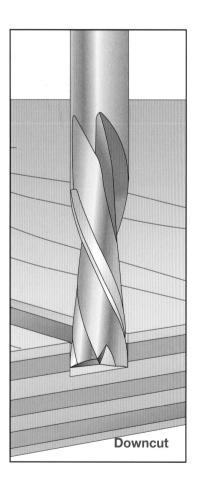

Downcut

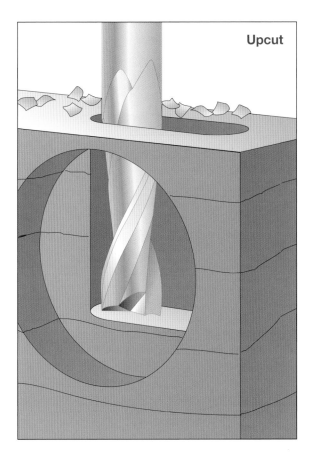

Upcut

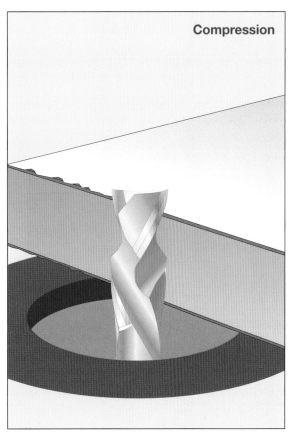

Compression

face up, such as jointing solid or highly figured stock. (Remember that in a router table, the upcut bit is now cutting down.)

Upcut/downcut or compression bit

The unique geometry of this bit cuts from the top down and the bottom up at the same time, and it's ideal for cleaning up the edges of hardwood, plywood, or melamine-coated particleboard (MCP). For such easily chipped materials, first cut the pieces oversize on the tablesaw, leaving about ¹⁄₁₆" on all sides. Then install a compression bit in the router table, and set the center of the bit's cutting flutes to about the middle of the workpiece's thickness. Finally, offset the outfeed fence ¹⁄₁₆" and joint away the rough chipped edges.

FLUSH-TRIM BITS

As its name suggests, the flush-trim router bit cuts the edge of one workpiece perfectly flush with the one to which it's attached. Those two workpieces could be plastic laminate and a countertop, edge banding and a cabinet, or a template and a rough-sized part. To accomplish this feat, the bottom-mounted bearing—so-called because of its orientation in a handheld router—matches the cutting diameter of the bit.

Note: *A pattern bit (bottom bit, above), sometimes called a "top-bearing flush-trim bit," also excels at duplicating parts. And, because the business end of the pattern bit is unimpeded by a bearing, it also can be used for dado-like cuts. However, this style of bit does not work for trimming laminate or edge banding.*

Flush-trim bits come in ¼–¾" diameters and lengths of ½–2". Better (and more expensive) bits have a slight shear angle to their cutting edges that imparts a much cleaner edge on your workpiece. That's especially important when working with solid-stock end grain or chip-prone plastic laminates.

Copy right

When it comes to duplicating parts—especially curved parts—you just can't beat a flush-trim bit. With this bit, the bearing and bit follow every curve of the template precisely. But before you can start reproducing, you'll need a part or pattern to reproduce. If you ever need to make

multiple matching parts, just make a pattern or template out of hardboard or medium-density fiberboard (MDF). That way, you can make mistakes in less-expensive material and keep precious project stock from the scrap pile.

Once perfected, trace the pattern/template onto your workpiece. Cut the workpiece to

rough shape on your bandsaw, cutting ⅛" or less outside the traced line. Bandsaw close to the line wherever you cross end grain. (Leaving less material here helps keep the bit's speed high and reduces fuzzing and burning.) Now, attach your template to the rough-cut workpiece using cloth-backed, double-faced tape.

Cutting across the grain can cause the bit to become grabby and may result in burning. Bandsawing your rough workpiece close to the pattern line on end grain reduces the risk.

With a flush-trim bit in your table-mounted router, set the cutting depth a little deeper than the thickness of the workpiece, as shown in the photo *opposite*. Rout the template/workpiece assembly, template side up, cutting with the grain as much as possible.

You don't have to make your own patterns, either. For example, when we need a zero-clearance throat-plate insert for our tablesaw, we double-face tape the saw's factory-supplied insert to a wood scrap of the same thickness, and use the same method with one exception: We set the bit depth so that the cutters barely clear the workpiece. That keeps the cutters from making contact with the steel insert.

Trim talk

Whether you're fitting solid-wood banding or plastic lami-

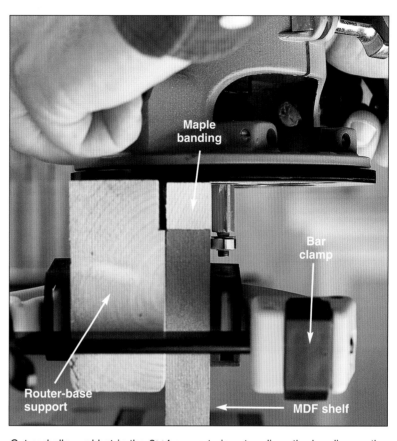

Cut a shallow rabbet in the 2×4 support piece to relieve the banding on the untrimmed side.

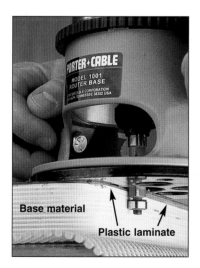

Keep the bearing in light contact with the base material when routing. Too much pressure can mar the workpiece.

nate, the process starts with one slightly oversized piece attached to another workpiece. How much larger to make the oversized piece depends on the material. For plastic laminate or wood veneer, leave no more than the diameter of the bit overhanging; for solid-wood edge banding, such as that shown attached to the shelf in the photo *above*, leave 1/16" or less.

The actual cutting is quite simple. Set your router's cutting depth to about 1/16" deeper than the thickness of the material you're trimming. Then rout the edge flush, working from left to right and keeping the bearing in contact with the base material below. Use a light touch to keep the bearing in contact. (Too much pressure can mar the workpiece.)

When working on the edge of a narrow workpiece, such as a shelf, you'll want to give your router base some extra support. You could always mount the shelf in your bench vise, and then clamp a 2 × 4 to the shelf, flush with the face of the maple banding, to keep the router perpendicular while routing the long edge.

STACKED SLOT CUTTER

If you need a slot, groove, or rabbet on the edge of a workpiece, you can't beat a stacked slot-cutting bit in your router or router table. This set of cutters with a single arbor gives you the flexibility to cut a range of widths, and you can micromanage the fit with a series of shims, much like a stacked dado set on your tablesaw.

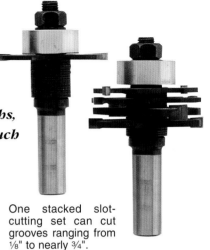

A stacked slot cutter can do things your dado set can't, such as rabbeting a curved surface, as shown *below*.

Mounted in a router table, use a stacked slot cutter to rout a spline groove in the edge of wide workpieces without jigging up a tall fence. For large projects, such as a built-in bookcase, mount the bit in your handheld router to cut slots for T-moldings or biscuits.

One stacked slot-cutting set can cut grooves ranging from ⅛" to nearly ¾".

How the cutter set stacks up

A typical stacked slot cutter consists of four cutters of different thicknesses (⅛", ⁵⁄₃₂", ³⁄₁₆", and ¼"), an arbor on which they mount, and a bearing that fixes the depth of cut (usually ½", although other bearing sizes are available). The set also comes with about 20 shims ranging from .1 millimeter (mm) to 1 mm for fine-tuning the cutting width.

The cutters themselves have two, three, or even four "wings," each with a carbide tooth on its end. Four-wing cutters produce the cleanest cuts, but are more expensive; three-wing cutters offer the best combination of performance and value.

Setting up the bit

To use a stacked slot cutter, figure the combination of cutters and shims you'll need to achieve your final cut width. The chart *below* shows the range of widths for each combination of cutters and shims. You must use at least a 1 mm shim between cutters, and the most narrow cut shown for each combo includes that shim.

Because the arbor isn't threaded along its entire length, you'll also need to add enough extra shims to reach the threads on the end of the shank. Put the extra shims on the empty arbor first, and then add the cutters and shims. Finally, add the bearing and arbor nut.

Remember to orient the cutters properly—when viewed from the threaded end of the arbor, the cutters should point counterclockwise. Mount the bit in your router and make a test cut in scrap stock. Add or remove shims as needed for a perfect fit.

Beyond the basics

Here are a few more tips to help you get the most out of your stacked slot cutter:

■ Forget to cut the rabbet to accept a drawer bottom or case back? Rout the rabbet in the completed box using a stacked slot cutter. The rabbet's corners will be rounded, but you can square them up with a chisel or radius the corners of the bottom/back to match.

■ The bearing also can be mounted on the arbor between cutters (say, to create the tongue of a tongue-and-groove joint) or before the cutters on the arbor for guiding from the top with a handheld router.

■ Although it's safe to use these bits in a handheld router, for stability and security you can't beat a router table.

Cutter combos for lots of slots	
Standard cutter(s)	**Slot width***
⅛	⅛
⁵⁄₃₂	⁵⁄₃₂
³⁄₁₆	³⁄₁₆
¼	¼
⅛ + ⁵⁄₃₂	¼ – ⁹⁄₃₂
⅛ + ³⁄₁₆	⁹⁄₃₂ – ⁵⁄₁₆
⅛ + ¼	¹¹⁄₃₂ – ⅜
⁵⁄₃₂ + ³⁄₁₆	⁵⁄₁₆ – ¹¹⁄₃₂
⁵⁄₃₂ + ¼	⅜ – ¹³⁄₃₂
³⁄₁₆ + ¼	¹³⁄₃₂ – ⁷⁄₁₆
⅛ + ⁵⁄₃₂ + ³⁄₁₆	¹³⁄₃₂ – ¹⁵⁄₃₂
⅛ + ⁵⁄₃₂ + ¼	¹⁵⁄₃₂ – ¹⁷⁄₃₂
⅛ + ³⁄₁₆ + ¼	½ – ⁹⁄₁₆
⁵⁄₃₂ + ³⁄₁₆ + ¼	¹⁷⁄₃₂ – ¹⁹⁄₃₂
⅛ + ⁵⁄₃₂ + ³⁄₁₆ + ¼	⅝ – ²³⁄₃₂

Note: Dimensions are inches.
*Variable widths result from adding shims.

BIRD'S-MOUTH BITS

Wooden boat builders have long used "bird's-mouth" joinery to construct hollow masts and booms. We landlubbers can also take advantage of this strong edge-to-edge joint, shown at right, when making cylindrical objects, such as columns, arched chest lids, or turned vessels.

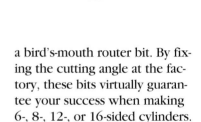

The bird's-mouth joint is better than a miter joint for a number of reasons. First, introducing the cutaway "mouth" creates more gluing surface; Secondly, the mouth cradles the mating workpiece, making it nearly impossible for the joint to slip out of alignment during a glue-up; and finally, you cut only one side of the joint, so you reduce your machining time—and chance for error—by one half.

A router bit makes the joint foolproof

Boatbuilders make the bird's-mouth joint on very long pieces using a tablesaw. As with any multi-faceted project, though, a tiny error in the cutting angle can become huge when compounded at each joint. You'll reduce your error rate significantly, however, when you machine your workpieces with a bird's-mouth router bit. By fixing the cutting angle at the factory, these bits virtually guarantee your success when making 6-, 8-, 12-, or 16-sided cylinders.

So, how many sides do you need? Ultimately, that depends on the nature of the project. The more sides in your cylinder, the smoother the curve will be. If you plan to turn the cylinder blank round, more sides also mean less waste because you can use thinner stock to construct the blank. On the other hand, if you want the cylinder to have an angular, faceted look, use fewer sides.

For a simple column, setting up to use the bit is as simple as the joint is strong. In your router table, install the proper bit for the number of sides (or staves) in your cylinder. Set the bit's cutting height to leave a small (say, 1/32"), flat bearing surface on the workpiece, as shown in the photo *left*.

After routing all the staves for the cylinder, apply glue to the routed edges, stand the staves

1/32"-wide bearing surface

Leave a small, flat bearing surface above (or below) the cutter for the workpiece to ride against the outfeed fence. This "rib" can be sanded or hand-planed away after assembly, or left intact for a decorative effect.

on end, and clamp them together with band clamps. If you have a lot of sides to assemble, a pair of scrapwood discs that fit inside the cylinder will help keep it round.

Think outside the cylinder

Want to be a little more creative? You can use the joint to decorate and "break" the edges of a case or chest, as shown in the photo *below*. Or, if you're up for a challenge, use bird's-mouth bits to create tapered cylinders or cones, like the ones illustrated *below*.

Things start to get a little tricky here, though, as the number of staves in the cone does not necessarily match the number of the cutter. (For example, the 12-side cutter can be used to cut cones with 3–12 staves.)

The fewer the staves, the flatter the cone—a 3-sided cone looks like a squashed pyramid, while an 11-sided cone is nearly a cylinder. You will need to do some figuring to determine the proper cutting angles for the staves. Detailed instructions and simple formulas for making the calculations usually come with the bits.

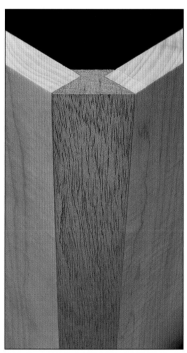

Use a bird's-mouth bit to soften (or highlight) the corner joints of a large project, such as an entertainment center.

BIRD'S-MOUTH BITS CAN MAKE THESE SHAPES AND MORE

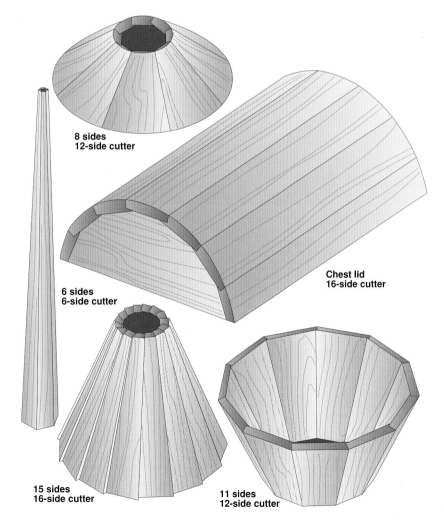

8 sides
12-side cutter

6 sides
6-side cutter

Chest lid
16-side cutter

15 sides
16-side cutter

11 sides
12-side cutter

7 Shop-Tested Router Tips

*T*he *"Shop Tips" department in every issue of* WOOD® *magazine is always a reader favorite. Why? Because it's filled with real, roll-up-your-sleeves advice gathered from both experts on staff and woodworkers like yourself (who often come up with some of the best tips). Often, these simple solutions to woodworking problems and helpful tricks that make jobs easier can be mentally filed away for use as needed. So, for this book, we've compiled more than a dozen tips that focus on routers and routing—feel free to put them into your own memory bank!*

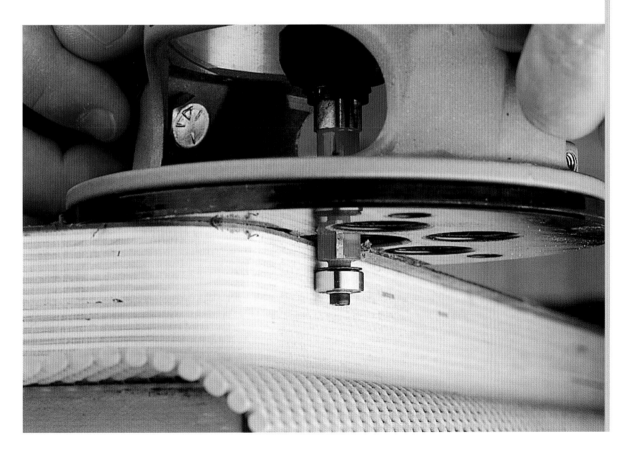

Dado routing made easier with a sliding tabletop

Routing dadoes (grooves across the grain) can pose several challenges, especially when you're working on narrow stock. Securing the workpiece, spacing the dadoes, and guiding the router straight over the stock become even more difficult on small workpieces.

TIP: A sliding top for your router table makes dado-routing easy. Start with a piece of ⅛"-thick tempered hardboard as wide as the front-to-back dimension of your router table and about 4" longer than the end-to-end distance. Attach a 1 × 2" guide bar across each end on the underside, locating them so the hardboard slides without excessive side play. Chuck the straight bit for dadoing into the router, and push the hardboard sliding tabletop into it, cutting a slot about halfway across the hardboard. Notch a 1 × 2" fence to clear the bit, and then mount it at the back of the sliding top. To rout dadoes, hold the workpiece firmly against the fence and slide the tabletop across the bit. Add stopblocks for repetitive cuts.

Shaving edges for gap-free joint

Say you're troubled by gaps along the mating line between the top and bottom parts of a small box you've just completed. Is there a way to true up the mating edges without resorting to a lot of sanding or planing?

TIP: This is a job for your table-mounted router fitted with a straight bit as shown at *right*. For each part, cut spacer blocks about ⅛" taller than the inside depth. Fasten them inside the part with double-faced tape. Then, place the part upside down on the router table. Adjust the router to take a light cut—about ⅟₃₂"—off the edge all around. Do the same for the other part. You'll end up with flat, true mating surfaces and a lid that fits.

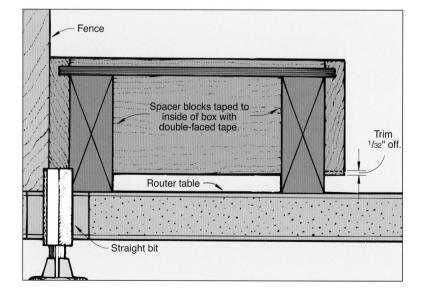

Fence

Spacer blocks taped to inside of box with double-faced tape.

Trim ⅟₃₂" off.

Router table

Straight bit

Your router can stand in for surface planer

You may need a small piece of thin stock for a project, but not enough to justify the cost of a planer. Or, maybe you have a planer, but the piece you want to plane down is just too short to run safely through the machine. Are resawing or hand-planing your only choices?

TIP: Put your router to work! With an easy-to-build elevated base, shown at *right.* Bore a 2" hole through the center of a piece of clear acrylic plastic or ply-

wood that's as wide as your router's base and about twice as long. Attach the router over the hole on top of the piece with the handles aligned lengthwise. On the bottom, attach a ¾ × ¾ × 12" cleat centered across each end.

Fasten the workpiece to a saw table or any flat, smooth surface with double-faced tape. Be sure to use plenty of tape, and tap the face of the wood lightly with a non-marring mallet to ensure a tight bond. Now, with a hinge-mortising bit in the router, adjust the depth of cut to skim off enough material to leave the thickness you need. If you need to remove a lot

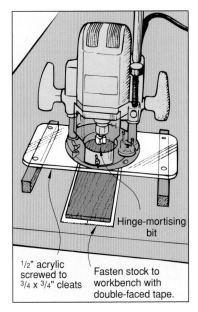

Hinge-mortising bit

½" acrylic screwed to ¾ x ¾" cleats

Fasten stock to workbench with double-faced tape.

of material, take it off in small increments.

Set up your router to zip round-overs on dowels

Sanding round-overs on several dowel ends can be a trying task, especially when you want the round-overs to match precisely.

TIP: Do the job with your table-mounted router. With a piloted round-over bit of an appropriate radius in the router, set the depth as you would for rounding-over any edge. Then, clamp a fence to the table with the distance to the center of the bit equal to half the dowel's diameter,

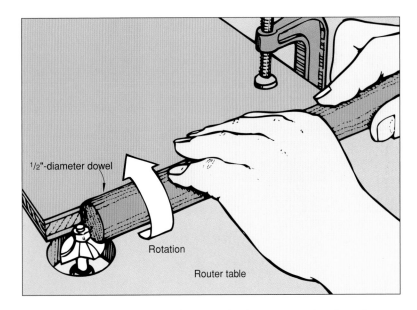

½"-diameter dowel

Rotation

Router table

as shown *above.* Turn on the router, and then slide the dowel along the fence into

the bit. Rotate the dowel to form a perfect round-over.

Use your router to make wide-diameter holes

A drill press and Forstner bit or circle cutter work great for boring holes with diameters exceeding 1". But what if the workpiece won't fit on the drill-press table?

TIP: Locate the center of the hole to be drilled, and with a compass, scribe its circumference on the surface opposite the face side. Next, bore a hole of the desired size in a scrap piece of ¾"-thick stock. Then, center the hole over the scribed circle and attach it to the workpiece with double-faced tape or clamps, as shown at *right*. Drill a starter hole large enough to accept a flush-trim bit for your router, and cut the final hole.

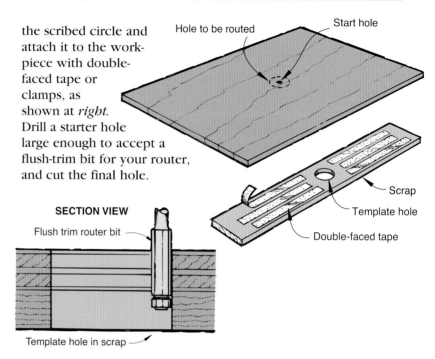

Hole to be routed   Start hole

Scrap

Template hole

Double-faced tape

SECTION VIEW

Flush trim router bit

Template hole in scrap

This long arm will lend a hand when you're routing edges

It's difficult to rout assembled box or drawer edges very well with a handheld router (especially inside edges). The narrow edge doesn't support the router properly, so you end up with a poor cut. A table-mounted router can get the job done, but what if you don't have one, or if the work is too cumbersome to handle on a table?

TIP: Build an extended base for your router from ¼" plywood and ¾" hardwood, as shown at *right*. The plywood width should equal your router-base diameter. Make it long enough to span your project.

Round one end using the router base as a template, and mark the mounting holes and router-bit opening. Then, drill an opening for the router bit. Drill and countersink the mounting-screw holes. Cut the hardwood stiffening spine, and then glue and screw it into place. Mount the router to your new extended base, and you'll be ready to tackle those outside or inside edges with ease!

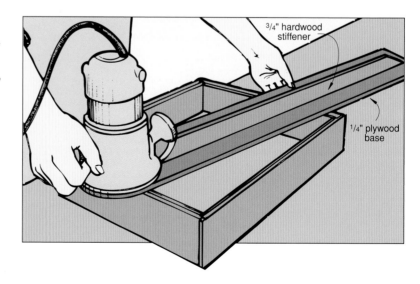

¾" hardwood stiffener

¼" plywood base

Cut quickly with a multiple-pass router

You like to make certain cuts with your table-mounted router in steps. What you *don't* like is reaching under the table to adjust the router ¹⁄₁₆" or ⅛" after each cut—it really slows down the job.

TIP: Set your router to the final cut depth, and then leave it there. Now, make your depth adjustments by laying several pieces of thin cardboard, artist's mat board, or poster board (all available at art-supply dealers and some crafts shops), or even ⅛" hard-board, on the router table. Each piece must be wide enough and extend far enough past the bit on each side to support your workpiece properly. Cut a hole in each piece for the router bit to protrude through, and secure the pieces to the table with double-faced tape.

Make your first cut with all of the shims stacked in place. Remove one for each subsequent pass until you've removed them all for the final cut. Each shim you remove increases your depth of cut by its thickness.

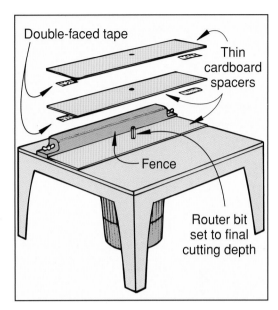

Double-faced tape

Thin cardboard spacers

Fence

Router bit set to final cutting depth

Simple mounting into a tablesaw

A table-mounted router simplifies many operations, but finding space for another piece of equipment isn't always easy.

TIP: Mount your router on your tablesaw. Simply attach the router to a piece of ¾" plywood long enough to span your saw's fence rails. Secure the table to the rails with ¼" U-bolts, as shown at *right*. The router fence clamps to the saw fence for easy adjustment. Both pieces can be stored in a small space.

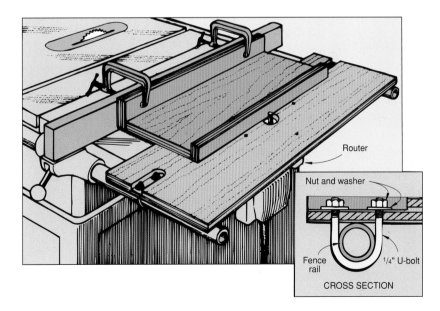

Router

Nut and washer

Fence rail

¼" U-bolt

CROSS SECTION

A router flush trimmer can help you "sand"

Particularly with today's thin veneers, it's tough to sand an edge band flush without sanding through the veneer.

TIP: This simple jig does the trick. Remove the plastic router base and screw on a piece of ¼" hardboard as shown. Adjust a ½" straight router bit flush with the bottom of the hardboard. Keep the router absolutely vertical and it will cut away any material that is not flush with the jig.

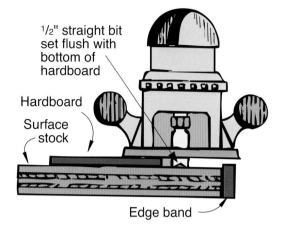

½" straight bit set flush with bottom of hardboard

Hardboard

Surface stock

Edge band

Tighten collets with one hand

A tight collet prevents your router bit from slipping up or down, and ensures safe routing. But sometimes those tight collets don't loosen easily.

TIP: When tightening or loosening router collets, you can gain more leverage with one hand than with two. Position the two wrenches so they fit within your grip. Now, squeeze the handles together to tighten or loosen the collet. This way, you won't bang your knuckles together.

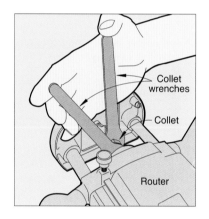

Collet wrenches

Collet

Router

Use your nail set to free stubborn router bits from a collet

When trying to change router bits, sometimes the old one won't come out of the collet, and you can't get enough of a grip on either piece to get them apart.

TIP: Hold a nail set against your benchtop with the tip pointing up. Then, put the open bottom of the collet over the nail set and push against the router-bit shank. Tap the shank end against the nail set until the bit breaks loose.

Nail set

This O-ring will prevent "Oh, darn!" when you're changing bits

Say the edge-forming router bit you're chucking keeps sliding all the way down in the collet, but it needs to be higher. Because both your hands are occupied with collet wrenches, you can't hold the bit in position.

TIP: Slide a rubber O-ring onto the router-bit shank, as shown, before you insert it into the collet. (You'll find ¼" and ½" inside-diameter O-rings in the plumbing aisle of your hardware store.) Position the bit at the height you want, and slide the O-ring down to the collet face. Now, you can tighten the collet nut while the O-ring holds the bit in place for you.

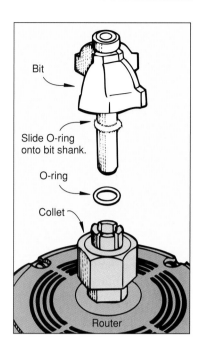

Bit

Slide O-ring onto bit shank.

O-ring

Collet

Router

Keep an "at-a-glance" profile of your router bits

Because the profile of a router bit appears to be the opposite shape of the cut it makes, it often takes a second glance to select the correct cutter for the desired shape.

TIP: For a reference of the bit profile, shape an 8" length of scrap material with each bit. Trim the profile to a shorter length and hang the profile near the respective bit. Hold the profile to the end of your workpiece before you make

any cuts. Be careful to always replace the profiles and bits into their correct storage locations.

A convenient flip-out router mat

Your nonslip router mat sure comes in handy. But when you roll it up to put away, you end up with a bulky bundle that can be hard to store.

TIP: Hang the mat out of the way over the end of your workbench. Place the mat near one corner, fold it over the end of the benchtop, and fasten it with aluminum carpet edging or countertop molding. When you don't need the mat, simply flip it over the end of the bench.

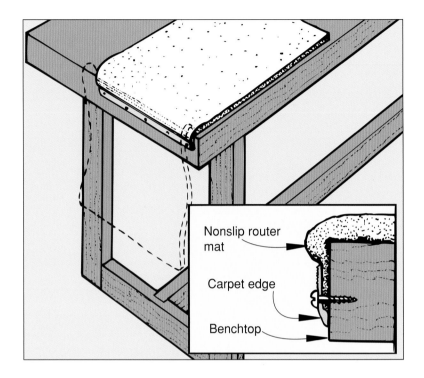

Nonslip router mat

Carpet edge

Benchtop

Store your router bits on perforated headboard

When using multiple router bits to create fancy profiles, the bits tend to clutter up your work area—unless you take the time to put them back into a case or holder.

TIP: If you're using router bits with ¼" shanks, you can simply slip the shanks into the holes of any empty section of perforated hardboard with ¼" holes. The shanks of the router bits will fit snugly and the bits won't fall out. If you use ½"-shank bits, you can drill a few ½" holes in your hardboard

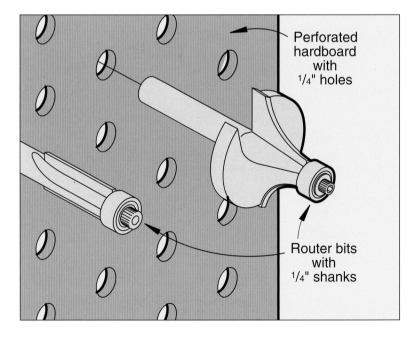

Perforated hardboard with ¼" holes

Router bits with ¼" shanks

near where you do most of your routing. Space these holes far enough apart so that the cutters on your bits don't touch one another and are easy to access.

Patterns Appendix

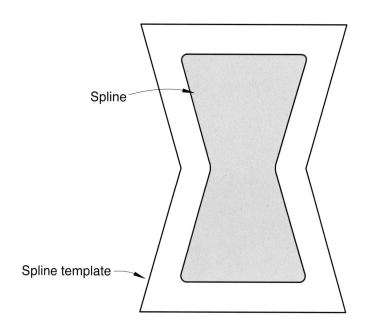

Spline

Spline template

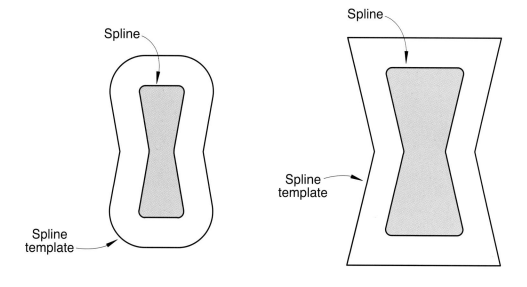

Spline

Spline
template

Spline

Spline
template

SEAT ROUTING JIG
Page 29

GUIDE RAIL PATTERN
75% OF ACTUAL SIZE
(2 needed)

Ⓐ

Location of Ⓑ

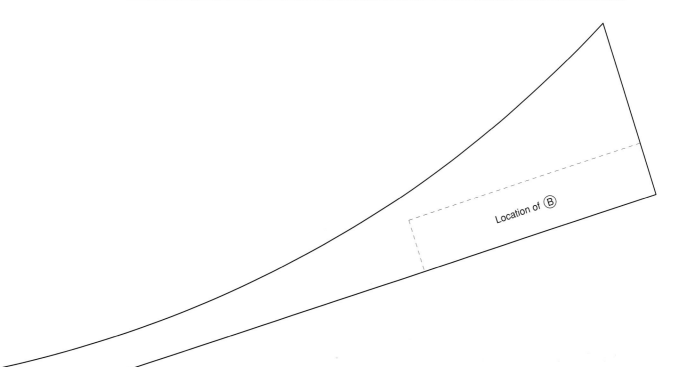

Location of Ⓑ

**TEMPLATES HOLE
CHARTS**
Page 54

HOLE	BUSH	BIT
2$^1/_8$"	3/4"	1/4"
2$^1/_4$"	5/8"	1/4"
2$^3/_8$"	5/8"	3/8"
2$^1/_2$"	5/8"	1/2"

HOLE	BUSH	BIT
2$^5/_8$"	3/4"	1/4"
2$^3/_4$"	5/8"	1/4"
2$^7/_8$"	5/8"	3/8"
3"	5/8"	1/2"

HOLE	BUSH	BIT
3$^1/_8$"	3/4"	1/4"
3$^1/_4$"	5/8"	1/4"
3$^3/_8$"	5/8"	3/8"
3$^1/_2$"	5/8"	1/2"

HOLE	BUSH	BIT
3$^5/_8$"	3/4"	1/4"
3$^3/_4$"	5/8"	1/4"
3$^7/_8$"	5/8"	3/8"
4"	5/8"	1/2"

HOLE	BUSH	BIT
4$^1/_8$"	3/4"	1/4"
4$^1/_4$"	5/8"	1/4"
4$^3/_8$"	5/8"	3/8"
4$^1/_2$"	5/8"	1/2"

HOLE	BUSH	BIT
4$^5/_8$"	3/4"	1/4"
4$^3/_4$"	5/8"	1/4"
4$^7/_8$"	5/8"	3/8"
5"	5/8"	1/2"

HOLE	BUSH	BIT
5$^1/_8$"	3/4"	1/4"
5$^1/_4$"	5/8"	1/4"
5$^3/_8$"	5/8"	3/8"
5$^1/_2$"	5/8"	1/2"

HOLE	BUSH	BIT
5$^5/_8$"	3/4"	1/4"
5$^3/_4$"	5/8"	1/4"
5$^7/_8$"	5/8"	3/8"
6"	5/8"	1/2"

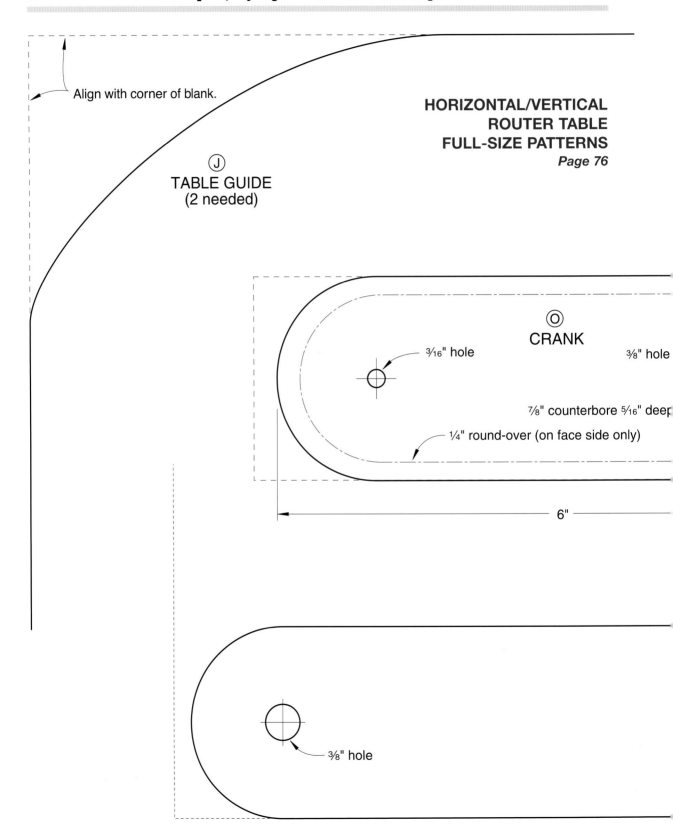

Align with corner of blank.

Ⓙ
TABLE GUIDE
(2 needed)

**HORIZONTAL/VERTICAL
ROUTER TABLE
FULL-SIZE PATTERNS**
Page 76

Ⓞ
CRANK

³⁄₁₆" hole

³⁄₈" hole

⁷⁄₈" counterbore ⁵⁄₁₆" deep

¼" round-over (on face side only)

6"

³⁄₈" hole

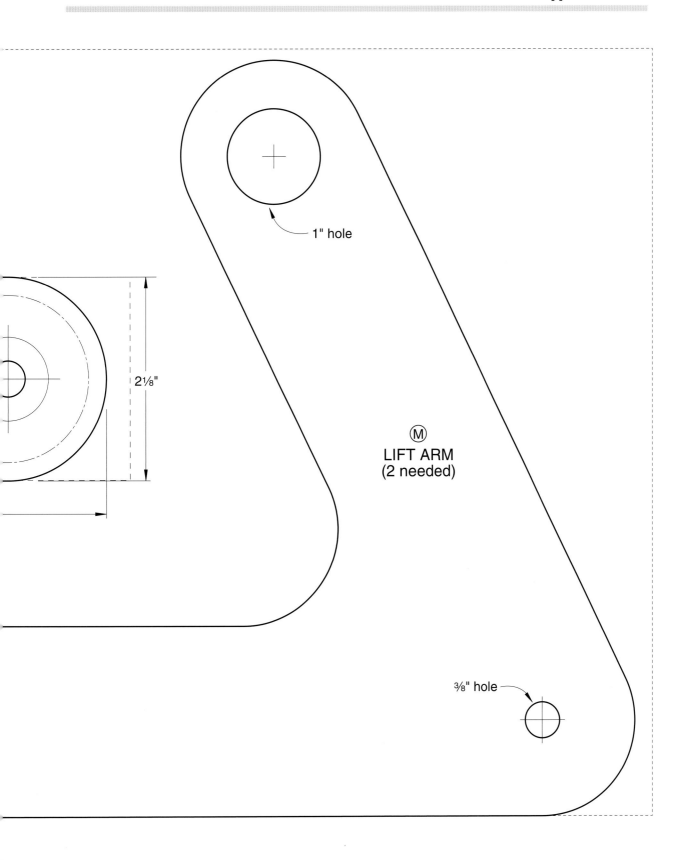

1" hole

2⅛"

Ⓜ
LIFT ARM
(2 needed)

⅜" hole

HORIZONTAL/VERTICAL ROUTER TABLE
PARTS VIEW—SIDE (INSIDE)
Page 76

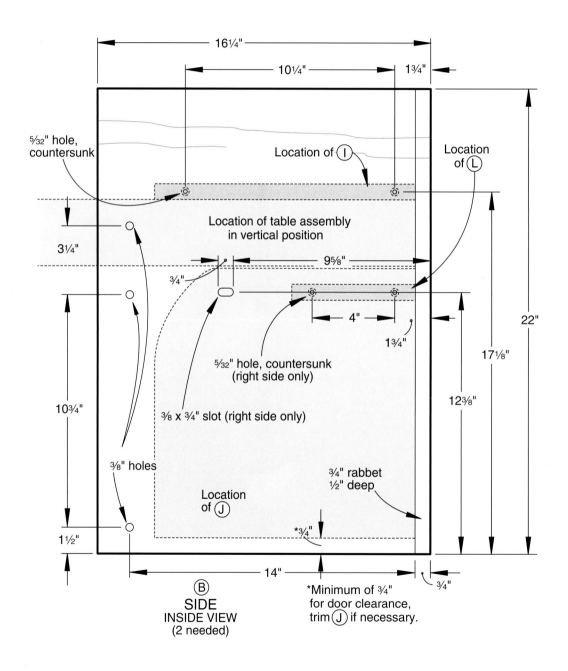

16¼"

10¼"

1¾"

⁵⁄₃₂" hole,
countersunk

Location of ⓘ

Location
of ⓛ

Location of table assembly
in vertical position

3¼"

9⅝"

¾"

⁵⁄₃₂" hole, countersunk
(right side only)

4"

1¾"

22"

10¾"

⅜ x ¾" slot (right side only)

17⅛"

12⅜"

⅜" holes

¾" rabbet
½" deep

Location
of ⓙ

*¾"

1½"

14"

¾"

Ⓑ
SIDE
INSIDE VIEW
(2 needed)

*Minimum of ¾"
for door clearance,
trim ⓙ if necessary.

HORIZONTAL/VERTICAL ROUTER TABLE
PARTS VIEW—TOP
Page 76

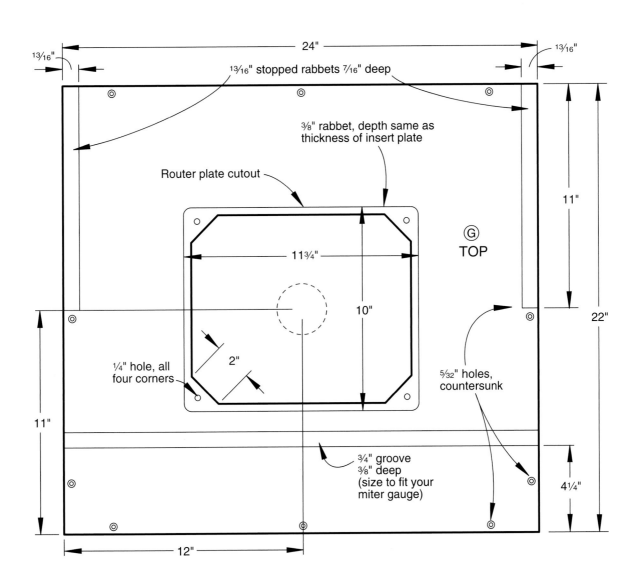

Glossary

A

Arbor: The part of the bit inserted into the router collet. It may also be called the *shank*. On an assembled bit, the lower part of the arbor also holds the cutter and pilot tip.

Assembled bit: A bit made up of several pieces.

B

Bead bit: A small rounded profile, available in numerous variations and sizes.

Biscuit jointing: The method of jointing wood and composite boards using splines shaped like oval biscuits.

Bit: The part inserted into a router that does the actual cutting. Bits are available in a multitude of profiles.

Box jig: A guiding device that involves the workpiece being held within a box structure for machining or drilling to a pattern.

C

Carbide tip: A tungsten carbide alloy brazed to a router bit's cutting edge to increase bit life.

Chamfer: To bevel the corner of a board at a 45° angle.

Climb-cutting: Feeding the workpiece in the same direction as the cutter. This is usually avoided except in certain routing situations (see *page 30-31*).

Collet: In a router, the sleeve that grips the shank of a bit.

Countersinks: Tools that cut recesses to receive bolts and screws with countersunk heads.

Cross cut: A cut that runs across a board, perpendicular to the grain.

Cutting diameter: The maximum width of the path made by any router cutter in one pass.

Cutting face: The cutting part of the bit, which can be either straight or angular (up-shear).

Cutting length: The maximum length of the full cutting edge of a router bit.

D

Dado: A square or rectangular recessed channel cut into the grain of the wood to house another board or member.

Depth of cut: Length of cutting edge of a router bit or, depending on how the bit is set in the router, the depth to which the tool has been set.

F

Flush: When two adjoining surfaces are perfectly even with one another.

Flute: The opening in front of the cutting edge of a bit that provides clearance for the wood chips. Bits may have one or more flutes, and they may be straight, angular, or spiral.

G

Grain: The appearance and direction of the alignment of the fibers in wood.

H

Hook angle: The angle of the cutting face in reference to the center line of the bit. Hook angle affects both feed rate and bit control.

J

Jig: A device created to help make specialty cuts with a router.

M

Medium Density Fiberboard (MDF): A special type of tempered hardboard characterized by a very fine, smooth finish. MDF is used mainly in cabinetmaking.

Mitering: The joining together of two pieces of wood usually (but not necessarily) at 45-degree angles, such as in a picture frame.

Mortise: A rectangular hole or slot cut into wood that will receive another member (called a tenon) to make a right-angle joint.

Moulding: A wood surface profile, or a narrow strip that is principally used for decoration.

P

Panel: A board set in a frame, it can either be below, above, or flush with the face of the frame itself. Normally seen in paneled doors and furniture.

Pass: One run of the router through the workpiece. Several shallow passes tend to give a better finish than one deep one.

Pilot bit: A router bit with a bearing at the end of the cutter that rides against the edge of the material or a template to guide the cut.

Pilot tip: The noncutting portion of a bit that limits the cut and guides the path of the bit by rubbing on the edge of the work. A pilot tip may be a ball bearing or a solid piece of steel.

R

Rabbet: A cut made partway through the edge of a board that is used as a part of a joint.

Radial relief: The clearance angle behind the cutting edge on the periphery of the bit that keeps the bit from rubbing on the work.

Radius: Half the diameter of a circle.

Rate of feed: The speed at which the bit travels across the wood, either by feeding the router into the wood or feeding the wood into the router.

Router table: Any routing system where the router is mounted in a fixed position and the operator does not manually handle the router.

S

Shank: The rounded part of a cutter clamped into the router and held there by the collet.

Solid bit: A bit machined out of a single piece of tool steel. In some cases, a ball bearing pilot tip is fastened to it. Solid, or one-piece, bits usually have closer machining tolerance than assembled bits.

Spline: A thin strip of wood fitted between two grooves to make a joint.

Stagger-tooth bit: A bit on which the cutting edges do not extend the complete length of the flute.

Straightedge guide: An accessory that attaches to the router base, usually supplied as standard equipment, that helps maintain the cutting direction of the router in a continuous straight line.

Subbase: An additional base fitted under the base of the router that helps in guiding the router in various ways.

T

Template: A piece of wood that's often made from cutting around a traced pattern that's used to route a shape in a board.

Tenon: A projection made by cutting away the wood around it to insert into a mortise to make a joint.

Tongue-and-groove joint: A common joint that joins wood in wood flooring and wall paneling in which male and female members form interlocking edges.

U

Up-shear: Another term for the inclined cutting face on a bit. The angle of the cutting face shears the chip in an upward fashion.

V

Veneer: A thin layer of high-quality wood bonded to a thicker piece of cheaper plywood to give the appearance of expensive wood (at a reduced price).

W

Workpiece: The board or component which is to be routed.

Index